The Origin of Strength

Sometimes the Hero We Seek is Ourself

a memoir

by

Dr. Eric Anthony Johnson

PIERUCCI PUBLISHING
ELEVATING WORLD CONSCIOUSNESS THROUGH STORIES.

The Origin of Strength

Sometimes The Hero We Seek Is Ourself

Published by Pierucci Publishing, P.O. Box 2074, Carbondale, Colorado 81623, USA

www.pieruccipublishing.com

Edited by Jonathan Grant

Cover Design by Muhammed Waleed

eBook ISBN: 978-1-962578-35-6

Hardcover ISBN: 978-1-962578-29-5

Paperback ISBN: 978-1-962578-30-1

Library of Congress Control Number: 2024912369

Pierucci Publishing books may be purchased in bulk at special discounts for sales promotion, corporate gifts, fund-raising, or educational purposes. Special editions can be created to specifications. For details, contact the Special Sales Department, Pierucci Publishing, PO Box 2074, Carbondale, CO 81623 or Publishing@ PierucciPublishing.com or toll-free telephone at 1-855-720-1111.

Contents

Preface

In the fall of 2023, I received a text message. I opened it up to see the picture on the cover of this book—me at age twelve, in my tuxedo with my big smile and my afro.

I had never seen this photograph before. In fact, I had never seen a single photograph of myself as a baby or a young boy…ever. Not one. That's just how things were for me.

So, I just stared at that picture in the text message. I somehow knew it was me; it was like seeing an old friend, like looking into a past life. Looking at that young boy, I just started to cry. In his eyes I saw a façade of happiness, masking the reality of stress and chaos that I knew was his life. I knew what that twelve-year old boy was going through.

I just kept looking at him, and in time, I got an answer to a question I had been harboring my whole life. The question I had been seeking an answer to, through all my journeys, trials, and triumphs as an adult, was this: what is the source of strength that has guided me throughout my life?

The answer came, and it felt as if a huge burden had finally been lifted. The answer was simple: the source of my strength is the younger version of myself—the iron-willed, instinctual, and determined boy who did not let the pressures of a negative and violent environment determine his life's outcome.

I wish I had the ability to go back in time—right now, as the grown man I am—and talk to that boy. I would simply say:

"Thank you. It is because of your strength that I am here."

Chapter One

Here We Go

I didn't follow the path that was laid out in front of me. Growing up in New Orleans amid the 70s and 80s urban decay, crime, and crack epidemic, even as a young kid I saw that road for what it was. There was a lot of pressure to comply, sure, but I found myself somehow immune to the negative impacts of my environment. I made my own trail—a trail that wouldn't have me falling for the trap or being on the nightly news with a bullet hole in my back.

I didn't follow the path that everybody was taking, not on the streets as a young man and not in the larger world as I got older. In short, I "got out." To do this, I had to think outside the box, to be disruptive in my thinking. And I want you to, too.

Whoever you are, wherever you live, if you don't agree with the status quo, get out and be you. Get out and do the great things you know you can do.

Sometimes you have to blaze your *own* trail. Sometimes you have to have the courage to go solo. Sometimes you have to be strong enough to *not* go with the crowd. It's not always easy, but there are times when we have to do it.

I mean, growing up it seemed like everyone around me eventually ended up in jail, struggling, or killed. That's the truth.

What gave me hope early on, funny as it may sound, was comic books. Then basketball, and then, in a really big way, school—education and even more education.

I knew I was making the right decisions, but I still got criticized for not taking the path that everybody else was taking. "Yo, Big E," people would say to me, "why do you want to do all this school stuff? You think you're better than us? Why you don't want to be workin' the streets like the rest of us?"

Because I knew there was more.

See, I moved somewhere in the range of eighteen or nineteen times by the time I graduated high school. My mom, my brother, my sister, and I—we were these "poverty nomads" constantly on the move throughout New Orleans.

I always wondered why we had to move so much. I wondered if it was because we weren't paying the rent? I wondered if it was because of bad relationships? Maybe it was because of all the chaos that was everywhere?

I didn't know, and I never really got an answer. We were just always moving to some new run-down place. So much so that it's hard for me to remember now where my roof was when something or another happened as a child. I have to trace my home back to the grade I was in at the time—every year in school I was living at a different place, if not two.

So, yeah, we were poor.

And all the things that went along with it.

My dad wasn't around, and my mom used to literally beat me and my brother up for forgetting to do things around the house. My brother wasn't exactly your "brotherly love" type of brother, and most of my male relatives were either drinking all the time, getting high, getting arrested, or getting killed. It was not an ideal environment for a child. Plus, I'd have to walk or ride the bus everywhere I went. That meant being out on the streets with the drugs and the guns and the predators and the thugs. I'm telling you, public transportation in New Orleans during that time was not a good place for anyone, let alone a kid.

But I had to get to school, and I had to get to basketball practice, so I'd be on the bus with all the older no-good types who were always trying to jack you. I'd ride one bus, change buses, walk a bunch of blocks, get on another bus—head on a swivel the whole time.

That was life.

Looking back, I see that a child should not have to go through these types of things just to get to school, the park, or the rec center. To me, a family should not have to live as poverty-stricken urban nomads moving around constantly. To me, human beings should have a good home.

It's no wonder I work in housing now—affordable housing. Because quality affordable housing was not something I knew as a child. It wasn't something I knew as a young adult. It's not something a lot of people in this country know about…and that has to change! Some people in this country have three or four mansions, while a lot of folks don't even have one single roof.

That doesn't sit well with me.

Everyone in this wealthy nation should be able to have an affordable, healthy place to live. It won't be a mansion and it doesn't have to be owned. But a roof over our head—*everybody's* head—is something that I see as a basic American right.

For all too much of my life, a good home simply wasn't a thing I knew. And that's why I've put in so much work throughout my life to get to do what I do now: help people and families find an affordable home.

They say that "no one escapes childhood unscathed." I know I sure didn't. I had to go through some dark times to finally see the light. But I wouldn't have done the things I've done in my life without all those trials I had to go through when I was a boy.

Whether it was fighting back at the bus stop when I was getting jacked by older guys; fighting kids from the St. Thomas, St. Bernard, Melpomene, and Magnolia housing projects (still have the scars to prove it) while at Kingsley House; being told by family members that I won't amount to anything; or proving people wrong on the basketball court or in the classroom, I had to make the conscious decision to *not* go along with what I was "supposed" to. Intuitively, I somehow always felt something just was not right about that lifestyle, like a gut feeling in my stomach. That's why I had to do it my way…see it my way…act and react *my way*. I didn't care if others didn't see what I saw or didn't believe in me. I believed in myself. Because if I didn't, I wouldn't be writing this book—I'd be in jail or dead or just laying around having not reached my full potential.

But I survived. I escaped, especially mentally, so I could survive. I escaped so I could thrive.

We owe it to ourselves to live our best life. I do. You do. We *all* do.

So, let's go, right now, on a journey together. I'll tell you some stories from my life and show you how I escaped a path that was no good for anyone—so I could walk the road that set me free to reach my full potential as a human being.

Just like we all can.

Chapter Two

Down at the Corner Store

W e had recently moved from Park Chester to Baronne Street. But even as our places of living changed, things stayed the same. And one of those things that stayed the same was what we ate. And let me tell you: we ate a *ton* of peanut butter and jelly sandwiches. PB and J after PB and J.

One night, we were out of bread. My mom looked at me and pointed a long finger. "I need you to go to the store, get some bread."

I obliged with a nod. Mom gave me a couple dollar bills and sent me off. It was summertime, one of those hot summer nights in New Orleans. I had on some blue jeans and a white tee, my sneakers, rocking my mini afro. The neighborhood grocery was only about a block away, and honestly it was nice to get out of the house for a bit.

So I walk on down to the corner store, the one run by the Korean family. The block is quiet, nothing much going on. I get to the store and walk around a bit, looking at all the snacks I'm not supposed to get. Looking at all the cookies I know we can't afford.

Just looking at all these sweet treats and thinking how good they'd taste. But we eat peanut butter and jelly at my house, and we need bread. So I walk over to the bread, pick up a loaf, and bring it to the register.

Standing there in the checkout line, the guy in front of me pays for his stuff and I see him walk out the door. I walk up to the register and am about to put the loaf on the counter when my eye spots something at the front door. This guy walks in. He's wearing a big camouflage jacket. I am on instant alert—it's summertime, hot as heck, this guy don't need no big camo jacket. My eyes go from the guy to the clerk, and I see his eyes get wide as he holds his palms up in front of his chest.

Then, boom. The guy in the camo whips out a gun. "Give me the fucking money!" he growls.

This moment is frozen in me, frozen in time. I can see it now as clear as I could see it then. The grocery store is set up like a lot of the neighborhood groceries we had back in the day in New Orleans. Behind the cash register area is a deli and then a door to a backroom. The clerk turns and starts screaming words in Korean toward that backroom.

He's just screaming at the top of his lungs. I can't understand the words, but I can feel the fear, the terror in his voice.

I'm twelve years old.

I am as still as a stature.

The clerk is screaming to his brothers.

"Give me the money!" the guy yells again, his arm outstretched and pointing the gun right in the clerk's chest. "Quit screamin' like that! Just give me the fuckin' money!!!!"

Screaming. Gun. Bam! Dude shoots the clerk right in the chest. The guy falls backward as the blood spurts from his body.

I'm twelve years old.

Still as a statue.

And I know he's dead.

For some reason, I look at the guy with the gun. He looks right into my eyes, this look that says *I could kill you so easy right now. So damn easy. And so you better not do nothing.*

I'm twelve years old.

I'm still as a statue—then there's a commotion in the backroom and the guy turns and runs out of the store.

He didn't even get the money from the register.

He just straight murdered that clerk and ran out of there.

Right in front of my eyes.

The clerk's brothers rush out the backroom with guns in hand but they're too late.

The guy's gone, and they go straight to tending to their fallen kin. There are screams. There is agony. There is pain and suffering.

I don't know what to do. So I grab my loaf of bread and walk out the store.

But I know I'm not out of the water yet. Still terrified. Still can't blink. I scan the area thinking that guy with the gun is gonna blow me away at any moment.

But I don't run. I walk. For whatever reason, I walk. Head on a swivel. Bread in my hand. That one-block walk is a marathon. I get home.

My mom glares at me. "Damn, Eric, what took you so long?"

I don't really know what to say. "Somebody tried to rob the store—and killed the Korean clerk."

"Really."

She said nothing more. That was it. She didn't console me; didn't even put her arm around me. She just made some peanut butter and jelly sandwiches and we went on with the night.

Chapter Three

Hoop Dreams

I still play basketball to this day, as a forward in the National Seniors and Masters Games. I actually play down in the age bracket where I face off against guys ten years younger than me. And I can still ball. I've won medals in tournaments all over the country, and I still love getting out on the hardwood whenever I can.

It's been a long journey with me and the roundball. It sure has. And though I've played for a long time, it took me a long time to even pick up a basketball in the first place. It didn't happen until I was twelve years old. A coach put together a team for the Biddy Basketball League, the historic youth league in New Orleans. This league has produced some great players over the years. It wasn't a guarantee I'd make the team, what with never playing before, but I tried out and the coach must have seen something in me.

That's where I got my start. We played at Sophie B. Wright Middle School, my junior high, with its old rotting gym, and we'd also play out at the Lyon's Center.

Right away, I knew I liked the game of basketball. The flow of it, the skills required for it. It just felt natural. I liked the feel of the ball in my hands. In short, I took to the game right away.

But it wasn't without a lot of help too. One day an older gentleman named Mingo saw me playing and came over to offer me some help with my shooting form. He taught me the fundamentals of shooting; how to get the proper arc and rotation. Then he just kept working with me, honing how I held the ball, how I placed my feet, how to release the ball "up not out."

I never knew if Mingo was his first name or his last name or some nickname he'd got on the streets; he was always just Mingo, and that man taught me how to shoot a basketball. He taught me a lot about life too, and about helping others. He saw something in me and when he took me under his wing, I developed a smooth jump shot, which was good, because at that age I was one of the smaller boys out there. I hadn't hit any of my growth spurts yet and it was hard for me to drive to the basket against the taller players. It was difficult for me to get rebounds or play in the paint. But with Mingo's help, I found my niche as an outside shooter.

The season started, and I was playing pretty well. I sank a lot of buckets. I learned to dribble well, to play hard and smart on defense. My team won a lot of games, and at the end of the season, to my surprise I was selected to the All-Star Team.

This was a huge deal to me. Not too much good stuff had happened in my life up until this point, so to be recognized as an All-Star was simply amazing. I was so excited, and so ready to play in that game.

But, sometimes it's two steps forward and one step backward. That's the way it is in life and that's the way it was in my basketball career. Because on the way over to the game, something happened. I ran into someone from my life who I rarely saw, someone in my life who I really didn't want to see.

I ran into my father.

Yep, just as I was walking down Louisiana Avenue, I saw him and he saw me. I don't think he planned on meeting me there. I mean, he wasn't around. There was no internet, no cell phones. He didn't know what I was up to on any given day. He had no idea why I was walking down that street.

He walked up to me. "Where you going?" he asked.

"I made the Biddy All-Star Team. I'm walking to the game."

He got this weird look in his eye, shook his head. "You're not playing in that game. You need to go home."

I was so confused. Wouldn't he want me to play in this game?

Apparently, he did not. No, he basically turned me around and walked my ass back home. He turned me away from playing in an all-star game? What was this guy trying to do to me? Was he trying to keep me down?

I was so incredibly confused. So incredibly and utterly disappointed. I never got to play in the game. Never got to show the other coaches what I could do against the best of the best.

It was a roadblock.

But it was also a springboard—because it gave me *motivation*. It made me want to try that much harder to be the best. Maybe deep down it was to prove my father wrong. Or maybe I just wanted to make another all-star team where he couldn't randomly intervene and turn me away.

Anyway, I doubled down. I started playing at the outdoor parks all the time, the one on the corner of Saratoga Street and Napoleon

Avenue, and over at The Drop—this tiny little half-court that sometimes had some good games. Basketball became my favorite thing to do, my driving force. We'd be at the park all the time; after school, during any breaks from school. In the summer, we'd be there from sun up to sun down just playing hoops, working on our game.

We all watched the NBA, and we all had our heroes. For me it was Julius Erving and George Gervin. I'd be flying around the rim imitating Dr. J's wind mills. I'd be out on the wing mimicking The Ice Man's smooth-as-silk jumper.

I did that all through the rest of middle school. Played all day, whenever I could, just working on my game.

By the summer before high school, I'd become one of the best players in my class. My shooting got real pinpoint, and the rest of my game caught up to where I was a pretty complete player.

By the time I was a student at Walter L. Cohen, I was ready to show the city what I could do. Ready to show that father of mine what I could do. And most importantly, I was ready to show myself what I could do.

But I knew it wouldn't be easy. Walter L. Cohen High School was serious hoops. You had to have the talent and you had to have the drive to play for that school. Plus, there was no freshman team so as a freshman, I'd have to try out for the junior varsity, which was mostly sophomores and the occasional junior. I worked on my game. I worked on my strength, my speed, my stamina, and my knowledge of the game. As the tryout neared, I was firing on all cylinders. Man, was I ready…

But then again—after those two steps forward, came a big backwards one. I was out on a bicycle one day about two weeks before tryouts were set to begin. I was racing against this guy, pedaling as fast as I could. We were speeding down the street and we clipped each other. I crashed—hard. I had flipped over the handlebars, and landed with a thud on my left shoulder. I stayed on the ground a moment then made it to my feet. I couldn't move my arm. Everything hurt, but I managed to start walking and made my way to my grandmother's house.

Grandpa and Grandma were playing cards. Grandma looked up and took one look at me. "We need to get you to the hospital," she said.

We went. Yeah, my shoulder was crushed—fractured *and* dislocated. They gave me a brace and not much more. I go home, and feel so upset with myself for getting hurt right before tryouts.

I mean, I was down for the count. I couldn't move my arm. It hurt to even sleep. For a moment it felt like all was lost.

Until I called upon Kung Fu.

See, I was a big Bruce Lee fan. I'd watched his movies—all of them—all the time. And I'd mimic all his moves. I liked what he stood for, how he would use natural things like a bowl of sand to strengthen his muscles. I liked how he was always saying things like, "Be water...."

So, I figured I'd give it a shot. I'd sit in hot water—as hot as I could make it, as hot as I could take it—and I'd just submerge myself up to my chin for long periods of time. All the while I'd be moving my shoulder around, trying out my "Bruce Lee method" to speed up the healing, and do whatever I could to get some strength and flexibility back.

You wouldn't believe it, but it worked. It wasn't magic but I really do think it helped. I got the shoulder to a place where I could at least run. And I still had my right arm. I mean, there was no way I'd be able to use my left arm to dribble or pass or shoot, but I could show up and give it all I had, one-handed.

The coach I'm trying out for is Alvin Gauthier. He's a great coach, very wel-respected throughout the community. Gets the most out of his players, does things right. And he's about as old school as it gets. He always held his tryouts at 5:00 am. School didn't start until 8:00 am.

We all know what he's trying to do, trying to weed out the serious players from those who stay up too late and don't prioritize the right things. Five a.m. for two straight weeks. I like it—I know I'll be there on time.

First day comes and tons of guys show up. There's so many people trying out that the court is crowded.

Second day comes. Still a lot of players, but less than the day before.

Third day comes and there's a big drop off in attendance. Only the serious players have stuck around. But there's still a bunch of guys out there and everyone's got talent.

Still, I knew I wanted it more than any of them.

Days pass. More guys stop showing up, others are cut by Coach. But day after day, I stick around. Even with only one good arm, I'm playing well. I knew I could dribble and pass with just one arm, and with how well Mingo taught me my shooting form, I find I can shoot decently even without being able to lift my left hand to help hold and guide the ball.

What really helped out a lot was—even though I wasn't big, I already had big hands. If I hadn't been able to palm the ball so well, I knew I wouldn't be able to play as well as I did.

Still, the competition is tough. Not many freshmen are still around. By no means do freshmen usually make this team. I'm only 5'9". A lot of the guys out here are way taller than me, way more built than me.

I don't know if I'm doing enough.

Then one day, Coach comes up to me. "Wow, man," he says to me. "You're doing all this with only one hand, it'd be fun to see what you could do with two…" and his praise fuels my confidence. I play harder, hungrier, and get better each day at playing without my left arm.

I'm doing what I can to show that I'm indispensable. I hang in there, keep getting to bed early and waking up early. Keep getting to the gym before 5:00 am. Keep playing my tail off. Keep being coachable, try to be a great teammate. Keep thinking about my father preventing me from making it to that all-star game when I was twelve.

Keep thinking about all those hours at the park working on my game.

More cuts are made.

I'm still around.

The final roster comes out.

Something like fifteen names—three of them are freshmen's names.

Mine's one of them.

And my father won't stop me from playing on this team.

Chapter Four

The Nuns and My Mom

When I was nine years old, in third grade, I attended Catholic School at St. Raymond, and there were nuns in the classroom. They were our teachers. They could still hit you with the rulers if you weren't behaving. It was a serious environment. One day, I really had to go pee. Like, I really, really had to go pee. I raised my hand and asked if I could go.

The nun said no. And if the nun tells you that, you can't go to the bathroom.

"My goodness," I thought to myself, "I'm about to pee myself! I can't pee myself in front of everybody!"

So, I made a decision. What the nun told me didn't make sense; it seemed backward, my pants would get wet and my classmates would laugh at me. The logic made no sense. So, I got up out of my chair and walked to the bathroom and went pee so my nine-year-old self wouldn't pee his pants in class.

Well, the nun didn't like that.

Nope, not at all.

She called up my mom, telling her through the receiver, "Your son does not know how to listen."

That's all my mom needed to hear. She dropped whatever she was doing and came right over to the school. She walked right into my classroom. She walked right up to me. She lifted me right up out of my little chair at my little desk. "So, you don't listen, huh?"—and she bent me over and spanked my bottom as hard as could be.

Right there.

Right in front of everybody.

New Orleans is a small town. It's a big town but it's a small town, and so you see the same people throughout your childhood all the way up through high school. And the kids never let me forget that. They never forgot Big E's mom coming into class in the third grade and spankin' him in front of everybody because he disobeyed the nun and went to the bathroom. Everyone remembers my mom trying her best to impress those nuns—punishing me for having to go pee.

I remember my mom, not having my back.

I've never forgotten it. That little nine-year-old is still in me, guiding me. Just like our younger, purer selves are still there within all of us.

Chapter Five

Lessons & Goals

S o, I made that junior varsity team with only one good arm. Throughout the year, my left shoulder healed up. I started to be able to use it well enough and have a solid year. I got into the starting rotation and played some good ball.

As a sophomore, I became a team leader and had a great season and I knew I was ready to make the jump to varsity the next year. That summer, I hit a big growth spurt and by the time junior year began, I was 6'5".

I tried out and made the varsity squad under the head coach—an older coach—named Coach Bocage. We got through the preseason and I was the only junior to make the starting lineup. My shot was smooth and my skills were evident. I felt good out on the floor and was putting up strong numbers in the games.

I truly felt like my star was finally rising.

All until we got to the district games. That's when Coach Bocage came up to me. "Eric, you are playing well," he said. "This decision does not reflect how you are playing. But for district games I want to start all seniors."

I was stunned. Shocked. I may have thought Coach was joking except for how serious his eyes and voice were.

It crushed me. The district games were the big ones. That's where you really got noticed. In New Orleans, that's where you made your name.

The next day, I was sitting in Ms. Hickey's English class. I couldn't focus on the day's lesson; my mind was reeling from the news of being taken out of the starting five. I mean, I'm sure Coach Bocage had his rationale for starting only seniors. Maybe he wanted more experience, maybe he wanted to reward them for their two years of hard work. I didn't know. All I knew is that it didn't feel fair, and it didn't sit right with me.

It felt like another step backward.

In order to take my next two steps forward, I decided to control what I could control. I got out my pen and started drawing in my notebook. I drew out my high school jacket, my letterman jacket. I drew out the outline of it—and then I started writing what I wanted to be on it this time next year.

I put:

#24 Eric Johnson.

All District.

All City.

All Metro.

I liked how those words looked on that jacket. That's how I want my jacket to read by the end of my senior year. It didn't faze me that only ten or so players in the history of Walter L. Cohen had achieved those three accolades in one year. I wanted to be the next, and I knew I could do it.

So, I wrote out how I would get there:

· *Average at least 18 points per game*

· *Average at least 11 rebounds per game*

· *Shoot 80% from the free throw line*

· *Team makes it to the playoffs...*

That was the path I laid out for myself.

Fast forward to my senior season. I'm the starting forward and we're rolling. I'm rolling, the team's rolling. I'm leading my team in most statistical categories. I'm well above 18 points a game (second in the league only to Perry McDowell, who's a New Orleans basketball legend).

It's late in the year and we're playing John F. Kennedy High School. They're a real good team, and they have two 6'10" twins on the team. The Twin Towers.

"I'm going to do something memorable tonight," I tell myself before the game. "Make a real impact."

It's a tight game, back and forth the whole way. Then late in the fourth quarter, we get out on a fast break. I'm trailing the play as one of my teammates goes up for a layup, but the Twin Towers are deep in the paint and force him to miss. The ball comes off the rim, comes off high. I'm charging full speed down the lane and I leap—I feel like Dr. J flying through the air—I grab the ball up high, above the 6'10" twins. Boom. I slam it down on them, dunk over them and they fall out of bounds with the force of it all. The gym erupts. People are jumping out of their seats.

I knew I'd just done something memorable.

We won the game. My coach comes running over to me, his eyes wide and with a huge grin. "With that dunk, guarantee you just made All City!!"

Next day, the newspaper comes out. It has the all-star teams listed. And there it is: my name's on all three of them. Eric Johnson: All District. All City. All Metro.

I accomplished my goal.

A lot of people couldn't believe it.

But I could.

And it felt good.

And it taught me a powerful lesson: the lesson of motivation, belief, and the power of writing out one's goals. I don't know if I would have achieved what I did that season if I hadn't been benched the previous year. That really firmed my resolve, and pushed me to work harder. What also motivated me was my brother saying how I wouldn't accomplish anything in basketball. I used the hurt of getting benched and my brother's negativity as motivation to form a plan and strive toward it with everything I had. It was a great lesson for me in my basketball journey—and a great lesson for me in my life's journey too.

Chapter Six

Captain America

As a young boy, my dad wasn't around and there were really no other positive male figures in my life. Not my uncles, not my older brother, not anybody I met on the streets. Comic books were my thing. Superman, Batman, Iron Man. Especially Captain America. That character's ability to forge through any situation made a huge impression on me. I saw his red, white, and blue shield as a symbol of strength and protection; and as time went by, I came to see my education, creativity, and innovation as representatives of my own shield that I was constructing.

So while I don't usually talk about this very much publicly, I was—and still am—a comic book guy. These super heroes were my strong male figures. Sounds weird, I know, but that's all I had. It all started one day at Kingsley House. Kingsley House is this historic building in New Orleans where poor kids like me could go and hang out, learn some things, and feel safe. It functioned like a rec center or youth center would in other cities. I spent a lot of time there, after school and during the summers and stuff. And it's where I discovered comic books. I remember it like it was yesterday: one day I walked into this room, a room that for some reason I hadn't ever been in before. I walked in and it was like a door to a new world opened up—from floor to ceiling, just rows of comic books.

My eyes got all big. I walked to the stacks and picked one up. Then another. And another. I read them all cover to cover, absorbing the stories, the images, and the lessons.

Man, I just loved these things. For some reason, I really started identifying with the characters. I saw the villains as the villains in my life. I saw the heroes as someone I could strive to be.

I started acting like them. I'd put a red towel over my back and jump off the bed and suddenly I was Superman. (Until I hit the floor, of course.)

Thinking back, maybe it was a sort of escape mechanism. Maybe it was childish. But maybe comic books were just what I needed. My life was so void of positive male figures that those fictional caped crusaders became my role models. The stories became my basis for moral-based learning. The heroes showed me what strength looked like, and what to do, how to act right, how to do the right thing.

And so, one day I was walking back from the bus stop after school, walking back to our apartment in Park Chester, and I saw this other kid—he probably wasn't more than eight or ten years old—getting worked over by these three older guys. These three adult-type guys were jacking him up trying to rob him.

It opened up something inside of me.

My inner superhero clicked on—and in a big way. I saw a garbage can and I grabbed the metal lid on top of it. All of a sudden, I have my shield. I'm not really thinking at this point, just going on instinct.

I ran over to the little kid and those three thugs. Ran over to protect. Ran over to fight for justice.

"Get off him!" I yelled, holding up my shield. "I'm Captain America!"

These three thugs just looked at me and laughed. I mean, I was no more than eleven at this point, these guys were probably eighteen.

"Get off him!" I yelled again. And I turned to the kid. "I'm Captain America," I said once more. "Run home!"

The kid looked at me and because the thugs were looking at me too, the kid had the space to get to his feet, and bolted away, running off toward safety. Then it was just me, my shield, and these three thugs. They were all older than me. They were all bigger than me. But they didn't know how serious I was. They didn't know all the angst I had inside me. They didn't know all the power I had inside me. So, I rushed these fools, started swinging around my aluminum garbage can lid like I was fighting some supervillain in a comic book.

But this was real life.

And these thugs didn't know who they just awakened.

I was full boar, full throttle. My eyes narrowed and I charged them with my shield. Though I was young, I was already strong. And though I was young, I was already fierce. These dudes' laughs turned to wide-eyed shock. I bulldoze into them with the garbage can lid. The thugs fought back a little but I didn't back down. I was going at it. I didn't care. Either I didn't care or I cared a lot. Still not sure. I was just swinging my shield and going crazy on these guys.

Those thugs could have beaten me if they stayed in the fight, but after a minute or two of feeling my fury, they no longer thought it was worth it. They knew that my garbage can shield could slash a forehead or break some teeth.

So, they said some stupid shit to me, then started backing off. Then they just turned tail and walked away.

I stood there holding my shield, and I felt like a legit superhero. And I liked it. Fighting for justice. Fighting for the little guy.

Chapter Seven

The Long and Winding Road

My senior year basketball season was one of those two steps forward moments for sure. I had dreams of playing big time Division I. But with the inhospitable climate in New Orleans at that time—all the poverty, drugs, and violence—major schools were hesitant to recruit there. The coaches just didn't want to take the chance of bringing any of that negative stuff into their programs. They really wanted you to prove yourself at the junior college level first. That was what was available to me, so it's the path I took.

I had two criteria. First, the school had to be out of New Orleans—I mean, I needed to get out of the crack epidemic, street gang stuff, and the decaying urban environment. I needed a fresh start somewhere. Secondly, the team had to be good. I got a few offers and ended up getting recruited heavily by a school out in Florida, Lake City Community College. They were coming off a great season, 29-3, and were ranked in the top ten in the country.

They were excited to have me, and I was excited to go. I trained hard all summer and got out to Florida in the fall, ready to make my mark. I was ready for another two steps forward.

But what I got was a giant step back. I got out there, and was playing well. No more than a few weeks after I arrived on campus, we were scrimmaging in practice and our 7'3" center, who was as clumsy as it gets, undercut me when I was in the air. My feet went out from underneath me and I braced myself with my hand so I didn't crack my head open. But my hand hit the floor hard. Bam! And I felt it right away.

My hand—my right hand—had shattered.

Before the season even started, I broke my shooting hand.

I was so dang upset. I thought about all the hard work I'd put in. I thought about everything in my basketball journey up to this time— Biddy League, making the freshman team, all the stuff I accomplished as a senior.

And I couldn't play. Because I couldn't shoot. I was out of the game before I could even begin. I'll tell you what.

Sure, I healed up enough to put a big ol' linebacker-type brace on it and play a few games that year. But it threw off everything. The wrist mobility wasn't the same. My shot fell off considerably. I was never the same. Not even my sophomore year. The ligaments and things never really healed during my two years at Lake City.

After I finished my two seasons there, there were no calls from four-year schools. No letters, no interest in me. I was so very disappointed. In myself. In my circumstances. In what I had to do next. I had to go back to New Orleans.

I went back home. It was hard—I mean even though basketball hadn't worked out in Florida, at least I wasn't in New Orleans. In some ways, I had kind of found myself by going to an area I'd never been before, and being amongst people I'd never met. It had revitalized me in a way, getting away from my family and all that constant crap always going on in New Orleans.

When I got back, things were in even more disarray than I remembered. It was the middle of the 1980s crack epidemic. Chaos was everywhere.

I didn't really know what to do so I got a job working at the Foot Locker on Canal Street. It was a really busy store, a really popular place. I mean, everyone was coming in there to get the latest Jordans, the new gear. I was a good salesman. I got folks the kicks they wanted. I got to wear the referee shirt, meet some cool people. I worked there for about eight months, and saved up some dough.

I remember I had Tuesdays off. This one Tuesday, I went and bought a motorcycle. It was my ticket for some freedom. I'd never really had a car, because I could ever quite afford one. But I saved up all my money from that job at Foot Locker and went over to this garage and bought myself a Honda 750. I proceeded to drive to my grandmother's house on my mom's side. When I get over there, she was outside working in her garden. "How you doing?" I say.

She looked at me sideways. Looked at my motorcycle. "You know, you're not helping your mom! Your mom paid for you to go to college!"

"Huh?" I say, dumfounded.

"Your mom says that you're not doing anything for her," my grandma said.

"I went to school on a basketball scholarship. My mom didn't pay my way—I gave *her* money to help out," I said.

"You know what, that's just not true," she said.

I couldn't believe it. I bought one thing for myself my whole life. I worked so hard and saved up all that money so I could have a motorcycle, and the first thing I get is backlash.

At that moment, I knew I could no longer stay in this environment. Junior College had given me a taste of a new start. I needed another one. I needed to get out of New Orleans and away from a toxic situation, and I knew it.

So, I joined the United States Army.

And though it was beyond hard at times (more on that soon), it was two steps forward for basketball.

Confused at how joining the Army could be a boon for someone's basketball career?

Yeah, I was too.

So, I was out in Germany serving my duty during the Cold War and one day the commander made an announcement: "We're holding tryouts for the All-Base Team. We will play a series of games against the German professional teams throughout the country. If you think you're good enough, hope to see you there."

My ears perked up faster than a skunk's tail. My hand had been feeling a lot better, getting its strength and flexibility back all through basic training and my time in the country. I picked up a ball for the first time in a while and went out and shot around. It was swish after swish, for real.

I decided to try out for the team.

I played really well.

I made the team, and was like, "Okay. Here we go again!"

I was in great shape. I was leaner than I'd been in a long time. And my hand was back.

We got to travel all around Germany playing these games against their pros. It was good competition. Basketball was just starting to become more popular internationally at that time. The USSR had won a lot of medals in the Olympics and teams outside the bloc were gaining ground quickly.

We would travel to big cities and intermediate sized towns and hoop it up. Sometimes the crowds would be big, sometimes not so much. Sometimes the gyms would be nice, other times not so much. Sometimes the refs would be good, other times not so much. But the competition was always good. And my team was good. And my play became very consistently good. In some games, I was flat out dominating, playing like I'd never played before. I was shooting the ball at like a 50% clip, I was dunking, blocking shots, making steals. It was a whole lot of gratifying fun.

I rounded out my two-and-a-half years in Germany and got transferred back stateside, to Fort Leavenworth, Kansas and kept playing ball. The only difference now basketball-wise was we were playing American college teams. Four-year colleges. My game was on point. I mean, I was putting up 35, 37 points in some of these games. Grabbing a ton of boards.

Little did I know, some college scouts started coming to these games. They weren't there *just* to watch me, but they were watching.

After some of the games, they would come up and talk to me, like, "You can really play."

I'd smile and say, "Thank you."

"Do you have any college eligibility left?"

"I still got two years."

"Do you have a B average from your last school?"

"Yes 'sir."

"You know you can get an honorable discharge, get into the Army Reserve or National Guard, and go to play on scholarship at an American university, right?"

"What?! No, I did not know that," I replied, but I liked hearing it, and loved the possibility of it.

I started visiting schools, going on these recruiting trips to mostly very good Division II schools like Salina, Kansas Wesleyan University, and Washburn University in Topeka, Kansas. I liked Washburn a lot. I got to know some of the players there, and liked the coach. Plus, they were fresh off the NAIA National Championship and made the jump to Division II.

"Eric," they told me one day, "we'd like to offer you an athletic scholarship to come and play for us."

I couldn't believe it. I'd get to go to a university—and I'd get to continue playing basketball. And I wouldn't even have to pay for it. I was in! I knew I'd never be satisfied with basketball until I fulfilled my dream to play at a four-year school. Washburn felt like a great fit.

It was great. Sure, it was D-II, but we were good. Every year we'd get to play some big schools like Oklahoma and Kansas. I got to play a lot as a starting forward. We won more than we lost. I got to play in front of some large crowds, in some big games.

One year, we flew out to California to play a big tournament in San Francisco. It felt like the big time just being on that plane—I mean, we usually rode the old bus from game to game. And here we were, some Kansas D-II team flying out to the West Coast. We got to the hotel, and this place was nice. I can't remember the name of it, but we were checking into a five-star hotel in downtown San Francisco feeling like Dr. J or Magic Johnson or something. I'd never stayed in anything close to this place. No one on the team had.

So yeah, we're feeling big time and that first night everyone wanted to go out on the town. So, of all things, we hired a limousine to drive us around all night. Now, it really felt like we were in the NBA. I mean there was an energy about it! And everyone was passing around this liquor called Sisco—a powerful alcohol that was well-known on the streets. Every time someone took a sip, it looked like their lips had just caught on fire. The bottle was going around hand to hand, the talkin' and the laughin' getting' louder and louder as we went from club to club. Everyone's getting drunk. There were girls. We were all dancing and hollering around. Club to club we go. All around San Francisco and over into Oakland. Bottles of Sisco disappear. We had a good time. That's for sure.

Trouble is, the team forgot about why we were in San Francisco in the first place. Forgot all about the game we had the next day.

So of course, the next day we went out onto the court and everyone's hungover. Everyone's sleep walking. Everyone's sluggish as all can be.

We get our asses whipped something awful. Blown out of the gym. It was bad.

The tournament went on and we got a little better but never found our rhythm. Some guys were still slow and sluggish three days after that first night. We didn't take care of business, and in a few days, we boarded the plane home.

We got back to Topeka at 2:00 in the morning. We thought we were all going to roll into our beds and get some much-needed sleep after all the travel.

Nope. The bus from the airport pulled up at the gym. Coach rips us bad for how we didn't get the job done. Then he ended with, "Get out on the court and get on the baseline! You're going to run until I tell you to stop. Get out there—everybody but Eric!"

See, everyone knew I didn't drink. My teammates knew it in the limo, and that's why I wasn't ever offered any of those bottles of Sisco. My coach knew it, and that's why he absolved me from having to run these 2:00 am suicides.

But I knew if I didn't get on that line and run, my teammates would never forgive me. I knew that if I didn't get on that line and run, I'd never forgive myself.

So, I got on that line too. And Coach ran us until we all almost puked. Then he ran us some more.

But I'd been through the Army at this point, I'd been through basic and advanced training. I knew that if this team was going to bounce back from our poor performance, it would take leadership and it would take unity. It would take everyone working together, bleeding together, doing it as one in a singular pursuit of greatness to get the job done.

That's why I got on the line that night. That's why all of us, from time to time, should step on that line, even when we don't have to.

I had a great two years at Washburn University, getting to play basketball on a scholarship brought me some satisfaction, fulfilling all my hard work to get great at the game since I was a young kid. All the way back to being 12 years old making that Biddy Team, and my father not letting me go to the all-star game; through the ups and downs of high school; the rock bottom of Junior College; getting to get back to finding my game in the Army…it had all been leading me here.

With all those two steps forward and one step backward, it felt like things had finally come full circle. Playing for Washburn University felt like completion.

Plus, it got me back into education. In a big way.

Chapter Eight

What to Do?

Growing up, there was this department store, this well-known place on Canal Street called D.H. Holmes. It was really big and seemed really nice. One day when I was about ten I was just walking past the store getting to where I was going, the bus stop on Canal Street, and this guy came up behind me and put a knife to my back.

"Ahh!" I screamed out.

I was a little kid. This guy was really strong, and seemed like a grown man. I could feel the point of the knife near my spine.

His voice was deep, "Go in that store and steal me a pair of jeans."

"No way," I said.

He dug the knife in a little deeper. "Oh, you're doing it, little man. I'm a 32x32, get me some Lee's. I'm gonna watch you—you don't do it, I'll kill your ass."

'Nother day in the life. I was just ten years old and I'm supposed to go inside and steal this grown-up thug a pair of 32s?

"Alright, man," I said. So, I got loose of the guy, took a couple steps away and looked back to get a quick glimpse of what he looked like. Then, I walked as calmly as I could into the closest entry point, the sliding doors on the corner of the store. I went inside, and started walking around like I was trying to find the jeans aisle but all I was doing was looking for an escape—some side door, some security guard, anything. Out of the corner of my eye, I look out the store through the big glass show-windows. There were a bunch of people out there, and I spotted the guy with the knife. He was pacing back and forth like some rabid dog. The words, "I'll kill you" were just playing on repeat in my mind.

My goodness. I walked around the store, looking for any way to escape this situation. "There's no way I'm stealing a pair of jeans," I told myself. "That's not happening. I'd be the one going to jail!"

So, I kept an eye on the guy, acting like I was looking for the jeans. I saw a bunch of people who just checked out, a big crowd of shoppers walking toward a different door down at the far side of the store. I got as short as I could while still being able to walk, hiding behind the racks of clothes making my way in a scurry toward that far door. My heart's beating like a hummingbird—bump bump, bump bump. I navigated my way through all the expensive clothes and finally made it into that group of people walking out the door with all their white-plastic bags. I was small enough to hide between them. Small enough to walk through the revolving door at the same time as a few of them. I slipped outside. I didn't know if the guy with the knife would be right there to meet me. Didn't know if I was about to get stabbed.

I made it outside and glanced over my shoulder. I saw the guy see me—but there was no way he'd catch me. I took off like The Flash, running down Canal Street for my life. I never looked back—and I didn't stop running for a long, long time.

Chapter Nine

From Wash to Wash

It's spring, 1990. I'm at Washburn University. The basketball season is over. For all intents and purposes, my basketball career is over. I'm in Kansas. I feel like I'm one of 142 black people in the entire state. I'm a Political Science major. I like my classes, but I don't have a clue what I'm going to do after graduation. I'm walking through the hallway one day, when something catches my attention on a bulletin board. It's this real official-looking flyer, great font, gold seals and such. It just looked like prestige on paper. I stopped to look at it, and read the words. *Presidential Management Fellow,* it reads. *If you want to set your career on an undeniable path, apply to be a Presidential Fellow.*

"Oh, Man!" I say out loud. "That's me."

It was like a light went on in my head—in my heart—in my life. I ripped off the little tear-off part at the bottom of the flyer and put it in my briefcase.

It sounded cool. It sounded like I could be the President of the United States or something. I really didn't know what it was, but I liked it. And whatever it was—*Presidential Management Fellow*—I wanted to be one.

I kept that little tear off piece of the flyer in my briefcase to remind me, so that feeling of "aha" wouldn't wear off. For the next few weeks, I would just pick it up and look at it from time to time. It stayed with me. I finally researched what it was—an elite-level program by which a civilian could get into the federal government. If you got it, it was a two-year appointment where you move to D.C. and the government throws a bunch of money at you to spend time doing research in a field of your choice. You'd get to spend time with members of Congress, the whole nine yards.

And get paid for it too.

I was all in.

"Whatever I have to do to get this thing," I tell myself. "I'm doing it."

No joke, before I saw that flyer, I was blind. I had no idea what I was going to do after I got my diploma. After I saw that flier, it was like I could see my path forward. Walking down the hall that day to my next Political Science class, right before I was set to graduate, I found my calling: Presidential Management Fellow.

I just didn't quite know how I'd get it.

After graduating from Washburn, I returned to New Orleans. No longer having an athletic scholarship, I needed money. This meant I needed a job. I thought it would be easy to find one.

It wasn't.

I knew I didn't want to work at Foot Locker again. I knew I didn't want to be a bartender or a dishwasher. I went to the unemployment offices. I looked into being a Sheriff. I looked everywhere I could to find a decent job.

What ended up working the best was this: before I left Kansas to head back to New Orleans, I had sent letters of introduction to just about every local politician. I informed them I had just graduated as a Political Science major and was looking for employment.

In time, I started getting responses to my letters and ended up finding work as a community organizer for the Local Initiative Support Corporation (LISC). LISC had been invited into the city by the greater New Orleans Foundation with the purpose of growing community development corporations—entities that would work to address affordable housing and economic development needs across the city.

I was beyond excited to get the job, and I got to do good heart-centered work. It felt like I was making a difference. As a community organizer, I interviewed local elected officials about the challenges in the community. The job went on, and one day Councilmember Jim Singleton recognized my name, having read the letter I sent now almost two years ago. Councilmember Singleton said to me, "Eric, we tried to contact you when we received the letter, but we couldn't reach you. We wanted to hire you."

We got a good laugh about it, and the work went on.

Shortly after working as a community organizer, I was provided an opportunity to work for the New Orleans City Council. I mean, the New Orleans City Council was the most powerful city council in the country, and I was working for it. Why was it so powerful? Because it's the only city council in the country that regulates their city's utilities. So yeah, it felt like the big time. I felt like I was on my way, putting on a shirt and tie every day, working with a good team, and going out to fight the good fight. I was proud of myself. I absolutely loved the work I was doing with constituent services, working on local ordinances and policy. It was probably the best job I ever had because it taught me how to navigate communities. Because of that job, I felt like I could go anywhere and learn the language—New York City, Los Angeles, Minneapolis, Annapolis. With the fundamentals and politic I learned working with the city of New Orleans, I knew I could go in and make a difference. It was a great job. But at the same time, I recognized that the work was not going to be conducive to me in the long run; the work was predicated on me "falling in line" to the way everybody else was doing things. This became especially true serving as the Legislative Assistant to the City Council President. Once that happened, my life literally revolved around this individual. And this very obvious fact kept popping into my mind: as long as he kept on getting elected and reelected, I had a job. If not, I would be up a creek.

It came to be that I just knew I wanted more. Needed more. I felt like I could have more agency, do more for myself. Better myself. And that's when I found a book—or rather, it found me. I was walking through the aisles of the Community Bookstore in Treme one day when it seemed to almost leap out at me from the stacks. It was a bold cover with a bold title: *Countering the Conspiracy to Destroy Black Boys*[1]. I picked it up. I started reading. I didn't put it down for a week. It spoke about the challenges of the African American male—some of the self-damaging things we were continuing to do to ourselves, and how some overcame it. I felt like it was written directly to me.

"My goodness," I remember thinking. "I got some catching up to do." I mean, even though I liked my job, I was living paycheck to paycheck. I was basically no different than the black males that the book talked about. And when I finished that book, my life was changed forever. Had a new beginning. A light emerged. Though I'd done some nice things in my life, after reading that book, I really saw that I'd been clueless.

---

1. By Jawanza Kujufu

If I wanted to become a Presidential Management Fellow, I needed to start doing things a little differently. I needed to put more arrows in the quiver of my life. I needed to double down on my education. I needed to double down on my self-improvement. I needed to go harder. So, I immediately enrolled in the Loyola University Institute of Politics. It was a six-month program that taught me so much about leadership in the context of local politics; I learned so much about myself and gained more self-confidence.

After that, I enrolled in the Metropolitan Area Leadership Institute at the University of New Orleans. I did these two programs while still working full-time for the city. It sometimes felt like there weren't enough hours in the day. But I knew I was on the right track. I was so motivated. I was learning a ton and building a bulletproof resume. I was going to get that Presidential Fellowship.

I then enrolled at the University of New Orleans to get my master's degree. But pretty early on, I felt that it wasn't quite working. This required my full attention, and in New Orleans—what with the job, the girlfriend, the family stuff, the lingering New Orleans crap that happened every day on the streets—it was just too much. So much was happening around me. I wasn't getting the grades I wanted, and knew I was a better student than this. I knew I could learn more, and learn faster than the baggage of New Orleans was allowing me to do at the time. "I need to focus on school," I told myself. "I need to devote more time to this endeavor."

And that's when I decided that I needed to leave, and get away from all the distractions.

Upon announcing I was going to move on, to my great surprise the New Orleans City Council awarded me a proclamation for my service to the city—and they named January 5th, 1995 as "Eric Johnson Day" in New Orleans.

I couldn't believe it. I was so honored, and more excited than ever to head off to further my educational journey. Of all places, I thought about Minnesota. It seemed a world away, and I liked that. Plus, I had an uncle up there who was actually a great guy. It seemed perfect—out of New Orleans, but still with someone I knew. I heard about a research fellowship that was offered at Minnesota State University. I put the work in on the application and got it. It paid the way and allowed me—if I could live on the cheap—to focus solely on school, so I could work on my Master's in Public Administration. One step closer to that Presidential Management Fellowship, that golden carrot that kept dangling out front of me, keeping me going. From the Dirty South, I was off to the Frozen North.

I got up to Minnesota in the Fall, and it was nice. It wasn't even cold yet, though I knew that would come soon. And it did. Still, it was a fresh start.

I needed a place to live. What I found wasn't much—some tiny, rundown, one room apartment. It felt like I could take four steps and go from wall to wall. But I didn't care. It was full of wild 19 to 22-year-olds who partied and drank and played loud music at all hours of the day and night like *Animal House*, but I didn't care. The windows were so bad that once it got cold, snow and ice would literally come right in through the cracks...but I didn't care. I could deal with the cold. I could deal with being the 30-year-old black guy graduate student in the sea of Caucasian party-crazed undergrads. Why? Because the place was right across the street from campus. I could walk everywhere I needed. And I knew I'd be spending way more time at the library than in my apartment.

I spent a lot of time in that library. Reading all I could. Studying all I could, doing research. All I ever really did at my apartment was sleep and eat breakfast; I pretty much lived on campus.

And I loved it.

My favorite professor was a man named Doran Hunter. He was a great teacher, a truly great man. He'd spent a lot of time in the defense industry working in Washington D.C. He taught me so much about public policy. He taught me a lot about how the world works too. He helped me out a lot and I loved his class, Public Policy Analysis. I learned so dang much from that man.

One of the most valuable things he taught me was understanding the public policy analysis method. It was being used in the Ivy League and other top-notch schools across the nation, and Professor Hunter could've written the book on it.

Which was good, because when I finally applied for that Presidential Management Fellowship, I knew I'd need it.

Near the end of my second year in the two-year master's program, I applied. I did all the paperwork required, which was a lot. It was a real formal process. They had you write some stuff out, you had to paper mail all your grades and transcripts and degrees and basically everything you'd ever done in your life. They did background checks on me. They looked at everything I'd done, who I was, at all those arrows I'd put in my quiver.

I walked down to the post office and sent out my application.

Then I waited.

And waited some more.

Then, finally, I received some communication and was told that I'd passed phase one. Big hurdle, and I'd done it. They invited me out to Washington D.C. for the second phase, the in-person interview. I was ready. Boy, was I excited. But I was nervous too.

So, I went out to Washington, D.C., for the first time. All them monuments. All that history. But I knew I was there to do a job, to do a mission. I knew I was there to put my best foot forward, to put all those arrows in my quiver to the bow.

I'm ready. I'm ready, and I know it. I feel great, know I am prepared and that I can compete against anyone.

The format is that these bigwigs are going to put me through a series of tests. In person tests. Though the movie *Men in Black* hadn't come out yet, it's not too dissimilar from what Will Smith went through to get into Tommy Lee Jones' Men In Black. I get there and they throw me into a series of exercises. They put me in a room behind a two-way mirror and have me do things, give me scenarios and see how I react, how I respond.

I mean, these were real-life scenarios, in-the-moment. Test your acumen type things. Test your mettle type things. And they were analyzing everything—what I said, how I said it, how I led, how I mixed with the other candidates in there. It was like an NFL combine for your mind and your soul. There was a lot of weight in what we were doing, and I could feel it. A lot of the guys just started talking real loud, it seemed like they tried to throw their weight around, be real outspoken leaders and show that they could be the guy. But I knew Lincoln. I knew Dr. King. I knew how Gandhi did his thing. I knew that the best leader isn't always the person that speaks the loudest. I knew that the best leader wasn't always the most brash, didn't thump his chest the most. I did my thing. I went in there and just was myself, used what I learned, just went in there like the political animal that I'd become. Yeah, you probably know Aristotle's

"Zoon Politikon," his famous term that man is a "political animal." Heck, we human beings got big white eyes that can communicate. We got high-level language than can communicate. We got body language that can communicate. We know what we got to do to get the things we want in life. We ain't solo beings—no, we're social beings. That's how we came to be at the top of the food chain. We live in societies. We live in cultures. Unlike snow leopards, we do things together. And all I learned from Professor Hunter, and all the other things I'd put in my quiver taught me what I needed to do: know people, know myself, act accordingly. I mean, it seemed like everyone there except for me was from Harvard or Brown or Georgetown.

But even though I was coming from lowly Minnesota State, I felt like I belonged. I sized up the competition just like I used to do on the basketball court. I knew I could play with these people. I knew I could hold my own and more. I went in there with confidence and knowledge.

And that's a powerful combination.

I wasn't trying to be the loudest person in the room or the most brash person in the room; I just went in there trying to be the most authentic person in the room.

I went in there to be *me*.

And that's what I did.

I felt good after those exercises, and then it was time for the written portion of the tests. They sat me down in a room with a pen and paper and asked me policy question after policy question. "Okay, you have x period of time to get y done, etc, what do you do?"

In real time, no computers, no access to any books or other research, just me and all the arrows in my quiver of knowledge; I had to write out my answers in essay form. It was grueling. But it was also kind of fun, like some great sports match where you really get to lay it all out there, all your training, all your grit.

Then, it was done. I stayed the night and headed back to Minnesota to wait it out and see if what I did was good enough. I mean, everyone there was qualified, some perhaps a lot more so than me. I thought I'd done pretty darn good, but I just didn't know.

Then this happened: the government shut down. It was the shutdown of 1995. "Great timing," I thought.

After a few weeks of not hearing anything (because literally nothing in any form of government was getting done), I went out and got myself a job. I got a job doing some community engagement work. It was a decent job, kind of a job-job. I was done with school, master's degree in tow, living in a little city called Burnsville outside the Twin Cities. The days become weeks that turn to months. "Man, I haven't heard anything and it's been over a half a year," I remember thinking. "I guess they're not gonna call me. Guess I was foolish thinking I would get that fellowship."

I kept getting up in the morning and putting my shoes on one at a time. I kept going to work. Kept doing what I could. One day, I got home and heated up a pizza. I sat down on the couch, turned on the ball game. I grabbed a slice and was about to take a bite, when the phone rang. There's no caller ID or anything like that back in those days. "Hello," I said.

"Eric," came a deep voice, "I am calling from the personnel department of the Presidential Management Program—and I would like to inform you that you've been selected as a Presidential Fellow. Would you still like to come out to Washington D.C.?"

I barely let him finish asking his question. "Absolutely!" I said, almost leaping up from the couch. "When do I need to be there?"

The next day I quit my job and off I went.

What started as the glimpse of a prestigious looking flyer at Washburn University had finally led me to Washington D.C.

Just like setting my basketball goals in high school, the value of goal setting once again proved to be effective. It became clear that though we may steer off course at times, as long as we have a destination mapped out, we can stay true to our journey.

Chapter Ten

Grunt

Before we get to my time in D.C., I feel like I must return for a short time to elaborate on my time in the army. Because let's be honest, I didn't just play basketball when I was there—and it sure was an education.

When I decided to go into the army, I had no clue what I was doing. All I knew was that basketball seemed over and I was back in New Orleans and the 80s crack epidemic was on nuclear levels. I was not going to be in that environment anymore, so I figured I might as well help my country in the Cold War.

I literally made my decision, and the next morning visited the United States Army recruitment center where I signed up, was tested, and assigned the role of becoming a supply specialist. Two weeks later, I rode the bus with my belongings over to the Mep Station on St. Claude Avenue, where I would start basic training.

They were happy to have me. Told me they'd call my name in a few minutes, and to help myself to the breakfast spread out on the table.

I went over and grabbed a plate. I always liked oatmeal, or at least that's what I was used to eating for breakfast. I spotted a big bowl of oatmeal and loaded my plate up with it and found a seat to go eat it.

I took my first bite. It was like no oatmeal I'd ever tasted before. I took another bite. One last bite. Yep, this was definitely not oatmeal.

I came to find out it was gravy! Some type of sausage gravy that just looked like oatmeal to my eyes. That's how naïve I was. I thought gravy was oatmeal. That was my first experience in the army. I mean, I hadn't even got my head buzzed down yet. Hadn't even got processed through yet.

A few days later, I hopped on the bus and headed off for basic training. The whole time I kept thinking to myself I had no idea what I'd gotten myself into.

I got out to basic training in Fort Jackson, South Carolina. It was hot as hell. This is where I will do all the grueling physical and mental exercises and emotional exercises to get me prepared to go to war. One of the first things I learned is how to take one piece of toilet paper—one single square of toilet paper—and fold it, over and over, into being able to use it, over and over and over again, to get the job done.

Yeah, I was in the army now.

They made you do all sorts of things like that.

But the hardest thing was that you were always together in a collective. If someone else in your platoon couldn't make it, everyone in the platoon was going to suffer. If your task was to disassemble your M16 and put it back together again in two minutes, your team was not moving on to the next thing until every person was able to do that. If three or four or even one person couldn't cut it, the whole group had to do it over again. And over again. Until everyone could pull their weight.

We had to run two miles in twelve minutes. So, no matter if you were the fastest person in the group, you were running those miles again and again until every single person made the time; as a unit together, you did it over and over and over again until Steve or Larry could finish. And so you'd have to learn how to motivate Steve or Larry to get it done. You had to learn how to be patient at times, had to learn how to get after someone at times, be encouraging, be a leader. You had to learn to pull your teammates along with you. You had to learn how to lead and how to get the most out of your team. The drill sergeants reminded you, over and over, that your "life depends on it."

And we believed them.

Plus, the food was just horrible. I mean, despite all the oatmeal I ate, coming from New Orleans, I was used to good food. Food with *taste*. And this gruel was horrible.

Anyway, I finished Basic and got my orders to be shipped out to Germany. This was the time of the Berlin Wall, Reagan and Khruschev, the Iron Curtain. I was to be stationed in Bamburg, a medium-sized city about two hours outside Frankfurt. I got dressed in my uniform and went to the New Orleans Airport where I flew to my connecting flight in Atlanta. I very nearly missed my flight there. They called my name, and held the plane for me. They literally carted me directly to the plane, and lifted the cart up for me to board through the door. They closed the door before I even sat down, and we were gone.

I landed in Germany hours later. It was a whole new world for me. A whole different planet almost. I looked around and felt my foreigner status loud and clear. But then a funny thing happened: walking through Frankfurt airport, I think I hear,

"Hey, Big E!! Big E!"

But I kept walking, almost ignoring the words. I mean, no way anyone knows me out here in Germany. But then I turned and looked. "Robert? No way!"

The guy walking toward me was none other than Robert French, a guy I played basketball with growing up as part of the Loyola University New Orleans Upward Bound program. It turned out that Robert had joined the army and was stationed in Frankfurt. We talked a bit and then said our goodbyes.

Seeing an old friend gave me a little hop in my step. I mean, I hadn't seen or spoken to anyone from New Orleans since joining the army months ago.

But, other than this little respite, I'll just tell you that the first part of my time in Germany was the hardest thing I've ever had to do in my entire life. From Frankfurt, we spent 30 days in a rural area called Wildflecken. It was one of the coldest winters ever in Europe. So we spent 30 days in the coldest, most miserable place of my life; out in it all day and night, training out in it, eating our meals out in it, even shitting out in it.

They'd have us do things like, say, pack up the entire base like you're going to war. Out in the cold! And it wasn't quick. Then you'd be in the convoy for hours getting to where you were supposed to go. Then you'd unpack everything, the whole mobile base, and set it up again.

You'd finally get done, after being outside all day long. Your fingers and nose and ears are frozen. But you're finally done and you think you can relax.

"Okay, now pack it up!" some officer would holler out. "We're heading back! Doing it again!"

You'd be so tired. So utterly exhausted. So cold. But you had to time to stop, no time to rest or get warm. It was so dang hard.

Having to constantly go through these drills, undergoing the grueling nature of them and learning the mental toughness it took to keep going, a lot of people couldn't handle it. And I'm not talking civilians; like, a lot of soldiers couldn't handle it. It was crazy. But they say war is hell. And we prepared every day to go to battle. Thankfully no one fired a nuke when I was over there. Thankfully, I never had to go into live combat. But all of that being out in the elements, all of that preparing for the Cold War to go hot, all of that always having to be prepared for battle at any moment—yeah, that definitely hardened me up. We'd be in the woods, out in the field for days on end sometimes. I cannot tell you how cold this German winter was. It was like snow and ice all the time. Not taking a shower for ten days, two weeks. Or standing out in the freezing rain trying to eat your shitty food. I was so skinny because of it all. I was my full 6'5" by then, but probably only weighed 165 pounds. I mean you could see my ribs.

But, having done it—having gone through that grind—it's made everything else in my life seem a heck of a lot easier. Even being in Washington D.C. amongst Congress and all that. Nothing was as hard as that winter in the woods in Germany.

Chapter Eleven
Balancing the Budget

I crammed the trunk and the backseat and most of the passenger side seat of my car with everything I owned and headed east. I left Minnesota and headed straight for my new life in Washington D.C. I didn't stop to see any sights on the road trip, I just tried to make time. I made the drive straight through, seventeen hours, only stopping for gas and drive-thrus.

I had no apartment pre-setup or anything, so when I arrived I headed to my buddy's house in Maryland just outside of D.C.—and slept on an air mattress in his basement for six weeks before I finally got my own apartment. Then the fun began.

When you become a Presidential Management Fellow you have to make a selection of which agency you want to be affiliated with, where you want to put your focus. It was a big decision because it would directly influence what type of work I was doing for the next two years. It was sort of like a recruitment, you'd go to various agencies and they'd give you a tour of the place, tell you what they did, how cool they were; try to woo you a little bit. It felt a little bit like talking to recruiters back in my basketball days. Anyway, I narrowed my finalists down to four: the Pentagon, the Department of Transportation, Health and Human Services, and the U.S. Department of Housing and Urban Development. All four had their aspects piqued my interest. I mean, with my military background, working for the Pentagon definitely held some intrigue. I felt like I could do some good work with Health and Human Services, and Transportation seemed to have a lot of upward mobility. But almost immediately, I felt called by Housing and Urban Development (HUD). It just totally made sense to me, what with Park Chester and all those places I moved around growing up. That was my origin. I wanted to better understand "the urban mess." So, I signed on with HUD.

One of the first things we did as a cohort was a very interesting exercise. It was led by a congressman out of Maryland. He tasked us "to balance the budget." *The federal budget.* I mean you often hear about it now and then, but in the 90s it was a true hotbed topic for the nation. No one had been able to solve it, not the career insiders, not Ross Perot, no one. We newbies were given four hours to do it. I mean, yeah, it was an exercise, we weren't going to present it to the House or anything, but in order to pass we had to find *some* way to do it. We could not come up empty-handed; we as a group had to come up with some sort of solution complete with how's, what's, and why's—and present it to the congressman.

Had I not been wearing a suit and tie; it might have almost felt like bootcamp.

What we quickly learned was that this was going to be extremely difficult. You had to look at the interest on the debt, which was a ton. You had to look at all the mandatory spending, which was a ton. You had to look at all the items in the budget for defense—that felt like a few tons. And then you had to look at all the big social programs: everything related to social security, to Medicare, to Medicaid, all of that stuff. We all started spitting out ideas—what should be cut, what had to be saved.

"We can't cut social security," came one voice.

"Well I'm not cutting anything in defense," came another.

"My mom's on Medicare," came a third, "so that's not going anywhere."

We quickly found out that finding a reasonable solution that appealed to all (or at least most) factions was going to be beyond difficult. We split into teams to divide and research. In time, we came back to report on what we'd learned. But in all honesty, we were neophytes to Washington and we struggled mightily. Just like the elected officials do year after year, we struggled to find real-life solutions.

The clock kept ticking and our four hours were almost up. "What are we going to present to the congressman?" I pleaded. "We need to present *something*!"

In the end, our big money-saver was to cut one of the big entitlement programs. It was a difficult decision. It was a difficult exercise. But it was a great introduction to Washington. It gave us our first glimpse into the reality of working with policy makers and the federal government. It was a snapshot hinting at the challenges we would face in the two years ahead of us. It made me feel like a rookie. If I were to work successfully at the federal level for policy makers such as Congress and the different agencies, I knew I had a lot to learn.

Chapter Twelve

Six a.m. at the Bus Stop

When I was ten, we were living in that apartment complex called Park Chester, which bordered the St. Bernard Housing Project, one of the larger housing developments projects in New Orleans. I knew no different at the time, but looking back it wasn't good. There was always this sort of predatory feeling in the air, where, you know, you're constantly on the lookout for someone wanting to do something bad to you: jack you, rob you, stab you, whatever the case may be.

And my brother and I, we used to have to walk to the bus stop in the morning. Every morning. It's how we got to school or uptown to Kingsley House. We knew nothing different. And, you know, school and Kingsley House started around 7:30 am, and with the connections we'd have to make, and the buses not being on time all the time, we'd have to get to that bus stop around 6:00 am.

Naturally, at that time, the sun isn't always up yet. Especially in the winter. You still got some darkness, some places for bad things to take place.

Especially this one morning.

So, back in 1974, the dress code in New Orleans was: a pair of Lee jeans, a cowhide belt, and a pair of Converse "Chuck Taylors." That was *the thing*. Everybody was wearing it. If you weren't wearing it, you wanted to. Those who didn't have it, wanted it. Human nature, I guess. So, this one morning, my brother and I were at the corner of Paris Avenue and Mandolin Street. Still dark outside, dawn not quite breaking in the east. And me and my brother, you know, we were clean cut guys. Clean cut children, actually. And out of the darkness, out of nowhere, come these three guys. They're not kids like us. They stroll up fast, all confident with a lean and everything. And they proceeded to come out of this dark pre-dawn nowhere and just jump us. "Give me your belt, nigga!" one guy said right at me.

I looked at him, this older thug.

I liked my belt. "No," I said.

Well, that wasn't the answer he was looking for.

"What you say?!" And he came at me with a fist.

I avoided the first punch, and turned my head to find my brother in my corner eye. But he was gone, bookin' it down the street and all I could see was the back of his Lee's as he sprinted away into the dark.

On my own.

Against three dudes.

Three grown men.

I'm ten.

No matter, I only had one belt and I wasn't about to give it up. Not to these guys. So, I swung back. I started fighting these guys. My brother's gone. Just gone and it's just me. No matter. I can be Superman. In an instant I snap into that character and start swinging.

Just goin' at it. Heck if my brother don't have my back. Heck if these guys are three times my age. I'm straight slugging. I'm straight getting slugged in my face. I don't care. My cowhide belt is my cowhide belt so I just keep throwing fists. I'm fighting these three guys—and they didn't quite know what they were getting into with this clean cut ten-year-old at 6:00 am at this bus stop. It's like some predatory fight out on the African Savanna. It's raw. It's survival. It got physical fast. I got hit in the jaw. I got hit in the stomach. I went down a couple times, but I got back up swinging even harder.

And after a few more blows—yeah, they got theirs in, but I also got mine—these hyenas come to thinking my cowhide belt isn't worth the black eyes or bruised ribs getting any worse.

"Yo, forget about this kid," one of them says. "We can go find some other punk wearin' a belt and take it from *him*."

Six o'clock in the morning. At the bus stop. Just trying to get to school or Kingsley House.

Just another day trying to survive

You know, my brother left me there with those guys, those predators. My older brother ran away like some gazelle but I stayed and swung like a lion. Had to. Only thing I could do. No other way. But when my brother ran away—I can still see the heels of his shoes as he ran—that was not cool.

Not at all.

No way.

Still, I fended off those hyenas. The bus finally came. I got to school that day. I learned the day's lesson. Tried to put all that 6:00 a.m. darkness behind me and learn some things that will help get me out of the 6:00 a.m. darkness in the future.

So I study. I learn.

At the end of the day, I said goodbye to my teacher and my classmates and walked back to the bus stop to take the reverse route back to Park Chester. I got off at that same bus stop where I got on that morning and headed back home. Back to my mom and my brother. I got inside the apartment. I saw them both. I figured my brother had told mom about it, figured I'm about to get a medal or something for standing up for myself, figured I'd get an extra peanut butter and jelly for not turning tail and running away.

I looked at my brother. "How could you leave me out there with those guys!" I said. I was hot. Couldn't believe my big bro be leaving me in the muck like that.

I also figured mom would help me out, have my back, tell my brother, "There's no way you leave your little brother behind when three older guys come and jump him!"

Nope. Mom was more protective of my older brother. Mom got on me. I'll tell you what. I was in the fourth grade, bro. Eleven years old. Three big guys come out of the predawn darkness out of nowhere, coming for my cowhide belt. My brother runs away, leaves me to fend for myself.

And mom gets on *me* for it?

I couldn't believe it. Still can't. But, hey, that's how it was and so that's how it was.

Chapter Thirteen

Four Very Smart Human Beings

S hortly into my time in the Fellowship in D.C., four of my other colleagues and I were given a great opportunity. We had the chance to have a sit-down with HUD Secretary Henry Cisneros. We were just government newbies, but this guy was the man. He'd been around forever, and was the former mayor of San Antonio. He had his finger on the pulse of community development in a big way. I remember walking into the room, nervous, almost like I was about to meet a rock star or pro baller or something.

We walked into the room and took our seats around the conference table. Secretary Cisneros was wearing a blue suit, white shirt, and red tie. It was supposed to be a no-pressure meet-and-greet. Still, I wanted to learn as much as I could and not embarrass myself. The whole time I was in there, I just kept thinking, *Wow, this is unreal. How am I even here?* I was so pumped, so excited. I didn't talk much, mostly just listened to the Secretary speak his wisdom. He spoke about how to get the most out of the program, how to make the best contribution, and how to do the most good. He's talking about public service. He's talking about fighting the good fight. It was like a pregame speech; I was getting goosebumps on my neck.

"Above all, take advantage of this opportunity," he told us. "Commit yourself and learn as much as you possibly can—so you can truly make a difference for this country."

I was taking it in, I was seeing my future. Cisneros was so totally aware of our nation's urban challenges. "As you work with cities," he continued on, "always work with an eye towards *creativity* in how you problem-solve. That is key. Yes, we have administrative rules. Yes, we have statutory regulations. But always remember the human being. Work from the perspective of helping the people. And above all, be creative in your problem solving."

I loved that. I loved that this top-dog Federal Secretary was talking to us about creativity. That got me so pumped. That was really important for me to hear. That was really a great lesson. Yes, there was a form; but within it, there was freedom to create.

I've never forgotten that advice. I've never forgotten that lesson. I keep that perspective with me to this day. Be creative. Innovate. When necessary, escape the status quo in order to get the job done.

As a Presidential Management Fellow, we would do what were called "rotations." They would send us to places across the country to work on special projects and expand our breadth of experience. On one of these rotations, I was going to be sent out to Kansas City. I'd never been there before. I was excited.

"How long?" I asked

"Three months."

That seemed like a long time, but I was in. Okay, I told myself, let's do this.

On that trip, I toured public housing and the Negro Leagues Baseball Museum. But my favorite thing of all was one afternoon, I had the opportunity to have a meeting with Mayor Emanual Cleaver. He was one of the few black mayors of a large city. I'd long been fascinated by black men in high-level political roles. So, yeah, he was a hero of mine. I was nervous to meet him, but I was also excited. I have always liked learning from people who have paved the way. And face-to-face is so much different than reading about them or watching them give an interview on TV It is just so much more powerful to be in the same room, to really get the feel of the person.

Cleaver was open and willing to give me a chunk of his time that day. I was curious as to why…I mean, he did not know me, I was just some young guy in town for a bit. But he did not hesitate accepting the request to meet me. That, in itself, was a symbol of genuine leadership to me. From one African American male to another, senior to junior, the gift of the most precious thing out there: personal time.

I arrived at his office and looked around, taking in all the photos and plaques and awards. I had another one of those, *Wow, this is pretty cool* moments in my head.

I had all my questions prepared, and had given them a lot of thought. I wanted his answers as to what is at the core of what great leadership was all about.

But he flipped the script on me. Almost from the get-go, he started asking *me* questions. I couldn't believe it. He wanted *my* perspective. He was trying to put me in the leadership role. It was fascinating. This pioneering black mayor was asking me, "Eric, what are *you* trying to do to problem-solve in communities?"

He asked me a bunch of questions. I gave honest and thoughtful answers. Spoke the words: "creativity…innovation…disruptive thinking…not falling in line with everybody else," talking about "not doing it for the sake of having a job but to truly make a difference."

I think he liked what I said.

After a while, he opened up. "This work is an on-going challenge," he said in his motivating voice. "One day, you have the answer, and the next day you don't."

"I hear you."

"Eric, to do this work you have to have strong mental fortitude. You have to approach problems your own way, solve them your own way."

"I will."

"There are a lot of needs in the city—and it's all about balance. You'll have to create priorities that some people won't agree with or will flat out reject," he said.

"I'm starting to see that," I agreed.

"Above all, be a human being. Work with the local policy makers, work with the city council members. Build coalitions. And know that it will be hard." He laughed. "I may look calm sitting in here today in front of you, but it's not always like this. It's all about having to have the ability to adapt, every single day, to what you have to do."

I was blown away by this man. He had wisdom, and he had presence. It was a great experience. I thought we were going to talk about policy, but it was more of a conversation about leadership. It was a talk about the overarching ways to get things done. I absorbed so very much that day, and will be forever grateful to that man.

Let me tell you this story from back in my high school days, back at a lunchtime assembly at Walter L. Cohen High.

There was an initiative sweeping the nation called Push Excel. It was a program aimed at urban schools and communities to speak to kids about the challenges of life and how to overcome them; about the importance of believing in yourself, doing the right thing, working grassroots-style in your community, and moving forward positively.

It was founded by Jesse Jackson. Yeah, that Jesse Jackson—the Civil Rights leader and political force that he was.

And he was slated to speak at the assembly.

I was looking forward to it. A lot of my classmates were too. I mean, even in the 80s, the Reverend was already a hero of ours for all he'd done.

I walked into the assembly and it was packed, jam-packed. There was an energy in the room. Jesse walked into a big standing ovation and started speaking from a podium in the school auditorium. He was talking about the Push Excel program; he talked about the importance of positive decision-making. He got onto the importance of school; about how detrimental it is to skip class and the negative effects of drugs and alcohol. He spoke about how that other stuff—skipping class and using drugs—has become so prevalent in the urban youth and gets in the way of going where you want to go in this life.

Then he halted his speech and sought out a face in the crowd. It was like he wanted to make an example out of someone. He scanned left and he scanned right. Out of everyone up in the auditorium, he raised his arm and pointed at me. Jesse Jackson picked *me* out of the crowd, looked me right in the eye. "Stand up, young man."

I was up in a flash.

"How many times have you cut class this year?"

"Sir, I don't cut class."

He shook his head, disbelievingly so. "Okay, well how often are you in the hallways causing problems?"

"Sir, I don't do that."

Again, he seems displeased. "How often are you utilizing alcohol or anything like that?"

"Never," I said, almost trying to quell a laugh because it seems like my answers are failing to prove the point he is trying to make. "I don't do that. That stuff doesn't interest me."

I think he thought I was lying. He kind of raised his voice. "Okay, sit down!"

And while I have the utmost respect for that man—I did then and I do now—you could just see the other faces in the crowd being like, "Sorry, Reverend Jackson, but you called on the wrong person."

I still get a good laugh about that day from time to time.

Fast forward about fifteen years. It's 1997. I'm doing my thing as a Fellow in D.C. I'm walking by Capitol Hill. I look up. Low and behold, I see none other than Jesse Jackson crossing the street. I grinned a smile and walked up to him offering a handshake. "Hey, Mr. Jackson, how you doin?"

He looked up at me and smiled. "Hello, young man. How are you doing?"

"Good, good. Hey, I don't know if you remember me," I started off real confident, but then got some nerves. "But, uh, you came to my high school once in New Orleans. At an assembly. You called on me and it was, uh, well, it got kind of intense…"

"Is that so?"

I respected this civil rights icon too much to remind him of how he growled, "sit down!" at me.

Anyway, we said our goodbyes and off we went. I don't think he remembered me, but it is still a humorous moment for me to this day.

Anytime I see Reverend Jackson show up on TV, I get a laugh. I have the utmost respect for that man. And I just thought it was one of those hilarious full-circle life things. And if he did remember, maybe I finally showed him that I was answering his questions back in the day with the utmost honesty.

As civil rights leaders go, there's Dr. Martin Luther King Jr. and the Reverend Jesse Jackson—and then there's the Honorable Andrew Young. Andrew Young is a former mayor of Atlanta and a former Ambassador to the United Nations.

Growing up I knew of him, studied him, and remember just being so amazed at his accomplishments. He had worked endlessly for African American equality in terms of education, human rights, and serving his fellow man. I took it to heart, and took his example and advice seriously.

While attending a conference in Atlanta in the early 2000s, I was walking through the lobby of the hotel where the events were being held. It was about 7:30 am, and I was heading to breakfast and getting ready for my panel discussion when I glanced to my right. I couldn't believe it. It was none other than Andrew Young, just sitting peacefully on a sofa. He looked great, full of energy.

I stopped and just looked at him. Needless to say, I was blown away. "Wow," I kept saying to myself. "Wow."

I really want to go over and say hi. So after getting my nerve up, I walked over and introduced myself. "It's an honor to meet you," I said.

He smiled with his eyes. "Nice to meet you, young man."

He proceeded to invite me to take a seat for a few minutes. The "few minutes" turned into almost an hour. It was amazing, just sitting there talking with one of my heroes. I can't remember how the conversation started, but I do remember Mr. Young talking about the challenges and tireless energy needed during the Civil Rights Movement during the late 1950s and 1960s. The way he spoke was mesmerizing; both in content and delivery.

He ended our conversation with something that caught me as peculiar. He detailed how the comedian and fellow civil rights activist Dick Gregory would tell him and Dr. King to "make sure you take your daily vitamins."

Smiling as he's telling me this, Mr. Young reaches into his pocket and pulls out a handful of vitamins and plops one into his mouth. "Not everyone listened to Mr. Gregory, but I did—and I'm still going strong!"

I feel like Mr. Young must have sensed something in me, like maybe I was working too hard and not taking care of myself. But heck yeah, the ability to get out of bed and be fully healthy is pretty dang important in pursuing your goals. So, to this day, based on that amazing interaction in the hotel lobby with the Honorable Andrew Young, I take a daily regimen of vitamins. It was some of the best advice I ever received in my life.

Chapter Fourteen

Black Churches

I had the opportunity to work on pretty specific, special projects during my fellowship. One of the most interesting ones for me involved a bad phenomenon that started happening in the mid-90s. Black churches started getting burned. I mean, on some level it had always happened—but this was like an epidemic. A lot of arson, almost like some new fad or something. It was mostly happening in the South. It got so bad, so prevalent, that Congress passed a bill called The Church Arson Prevention Act.

A lot of money was going to be put into the rebuilding process. But in order to get the money to the right people for the right reasons, conversations needed to be had. In-person conversations. Human-to-human conversations. Interviews with the church leaders had to be set up with people in government to figure out exactly what each church needed on a case-by-case basis.

It was a big deal, and I wanted in on it. I'd always been interested in black churches. Curious about them. I mean, wherever I went, it seemed churches were the hub of the community. I knew, firsthand, their vital role in the community. I was familiar with the reason for their creation and I was familiar with the challenges they faced. I'd even written my graduate school thesis on black churches as an economic institution. I'd done my research both as a black man who'd gone to church his whole life, and then in books, studies, and documents. I became well-versed on the subject. This made me an ideal candidate to talk with the church leaders.

Which meant I was hopping on a plane. Or several.

I flew all over. I went to Alabama, South Carolina, Georgia, and Louisiana. It was boots on the ground. I was out on the front line doing my best to figure out the best possible path forward for all involved.

Most of the churches that had been burned were out in rural areas. The churches had largely been the social and spiritual centers of these places, hubs for all sorts of activities. I'd go there, talk to the pastors. I'd talk to the people of the congregations. The FBI was out there too doing their investigations into what had happened. I was there to figure out what to do from this point forward.

From the get-go, I was taken aback by the devastation of the fires. Most of the churches were simply wiped out, nothing but black rubble and ash. I also saw that these churches were not financially strong; it was obvious that without proper allocation of the funds that the rebuilding efforts would be a real problem. The situation looked dire. I kept asking myself, *would they ever get rebuilt? Would the people in these communities have a place to gather?*

I got to know people. I got to know communities. It felt like good, solid work. I would gather my information, tabulate it out, and send my findings back to HUD in the form of a policy brief. The folks back in Washington would read my report and begin to align resources.

I had high hopes.

But honestly, it was a tough situation. The feeling I got from the ministers and people in these rural communities was something like, "the federal government was going to (finally) do something and come in and save the day. Tons of money and cranes and crews would show up and, in no time, new churches would spring forth from the ashes."

Unfortunately, that wasn't the case. See, the Arson Prevention Act was a loan-guarantee program. In short, that meant that only if the churches could get their finances up to a certain place would they get granted a loan. If a church's finances weren't in order, they wouldn't qualify for the loan.

"I don't get it," I kept hearing over and over. "Why can't they just give us the money?"

Yep, there was a lot of confusion. A lot of confusion and disappointment. Frustration ran high—and I don't blame the communities one bit.

It all came down to allocation. It all came down to budgeting. And this meant that a lot of the burned-church communities didn't get what they needed for a successful rebuild. It was an early education for me into the red tape of federal resources. Yes, a lot of money was provided for by that bill—but nearly no one got enough of it.

I gave a lot of heart and soul to that project. I gave a lot of blood, sweat, and tears. While I was able to help out how I could, I always wished I was able to do more. I always wished I could have truly been a superhero for all of those communities, get all those churches rebuilt in a flash.

Sadly, I was learning that just wasn't the case with the federal government.

Chapter Fifteen

On the Way to Practice One Day

Even on my side of Canal Street, my rep would sometimes get put to the test. People still tried to drag me into the muck.

One day I was minding my own business, just walking, when I see these three guys with a pipe. "Big E," they called out to me, "come over here and get high with us."

I looked over and shook my head. "I'm six foot, five inches tall. I'm high enough."

"Ah, you soft."

I shook my head again, tried to keep walking.

"Come on, Big E, come hit this pipe."

"I'm going to practice," I said.

"Ah, you soft."

I looked at them again. Wasn't sure whether to laugh or cry. I stopped walking, kept my face like stone. "Tell you what," I said. "In 20 years, let's see where you're at—and let's see where I'm at."

They just laughed.

No joke, 20 years later all three of those guys were either dead or in jail.

And I wasn't.

It was like I had a guardian angel or something. Or maybe it was my will. Maybe I really liked proving people wrong or maybe I was just lucky. I don't know—I just carved my own path. I did, and kept doing. Time went on, and I took care of my business. I stayed clean, stayed away from the drugs, stayed away from the chains that hold many black men down.

I remember going back to New Orleans in my 40s, seeing some of the old brothers, the guys who'd somehow managed to stay alive, some who'd gone to prison and gotten out, most of them just doing the same things they'd done when we were kids. I'd run into them and they'd look at me, just stop and look at me, me all clean-cut with my suit. They'd be like: "Man, I remember you said to me back in high school all this shit you were gonna do—damn, Big E, you did it! We used to laugh at you, you tellin' us all the shit you were gonna do."

And we'd talk a little bit, tell old stories, this and that.

And a lot of those conversations with those guys who used to laugh at me, those guys who used to call me soft, they'd end up like this: "Hey, E… you think you can help me get a job?"

And I'd do my best to see what I could do.

Because that's all we can do.

Our best.

And that is all we must do: try—our very best.

Postscript:

Those guys I saw when I went back home in my 40s weren't bad dudes. They weren't bad people. Heck, they weren't even bad dudes back in the day when we were all growing up and everyone was doing their gangster stuff. What they were, was simply a victim of their circumstance.

Yeah, I worked my rear-end off to escape the cycle of drugs, violence, and poverty that was New Orleans back then. But I also got some breaks. I also had support.

And right here, on this page of my book I'm just going to state this flat out:

> To support people who are working to overcome societally ingrained obstacles, we as a nation need to put greater community support systems in place. We need to do this in order to foster an environment where every human being is afforded the opportunity to reach their life's maximum potential.

There, I've said my piece. Now let's move on…

Chapter Sixteen

A Woman with Energy and Advice

As young individuals coming into the federal government, we were all charged with great energy. I mean, we were working at HUD for crying out loud. What an opportunity!

Trouble was, we soon came to find out that our enthusiasm was not matched by the rank-and-file workers throughout the department. It didn't sit well with them. We were young and we were hungry. They were oldish and jaded. We were bright-eyed. Their views were clouded with the decades-long wear-and-tear of governmental work. We were seeking creative ways to do new things. They were largely committed to doing the same thing they'd always done, in the same ways, and expecting different results.

Coming in, I mean, I thought all of these policy makers would have spent large portions of their career out in the field, boots on the ground, learning about the people in order to write great policy that supports the communities they serve. It was the exact opposite; when I'd ask them about it, they'd be like, "No, I've pretty much just been in this office for the past 20 years."

It didn't make sense to me. I mean, to make great policy you have to go beyond the books and get out there into the trenches!

It often felt like being a round peg being forced into a square hole. It felt like having a ceiling put on you. We were ready to change the world—and we truly thought we could.

We wanted change.

But everything around us seemed to want everything to stay just the way it was—even though myself (and a lot of other Americans) didn't feel like "the way it was" was working very well at all.

There was a diamond in the rough though. A career governmental worker who had been at HUD a long, long time. Her name was Donna Abernathy, and though she was in her 60s, she still had that gleam in her eye, still had that pep in her step. Donna was a senior executive at HUD. And I was just blown away by the type of energy she had, by the pace she had, and the levels of work she had achieved. I learned a lot from her; a lot about policy and a lot about human beings. A lot about life too. I found myself in the elevator with her one day. "Donna," I asked. "What's your secret?"

"What do you mean?"

"I mean, you have drive. You have passion. What separates you from everyone else around here in terms of your energy?"

She kind of smiled a little smile and looked me in the eye. "You know, Eric, my strategy in life is this: you give everything you can while you're here at work, everything you have. You go hard. You push. But when you're done with work for the day, you're done. You do not take it home with you. You structure your life to make sure you have that separation, that balance."

The elevator ride ended and Donna nodded a goodbye and walked out. And I was left thinking about what she said. It wasn't rocket science. It wasn't about government work or policy work. But it was great advice, and I just kept thinking about it. I'd been taking my work home with me for far too long. In graduate school, I never stopped. I was always working. During my fellowship, I was living it 24/7. I really had no life outside of work because everything *was* work. And so I made a vow right then and there to follow Donna's advice.

When I was at work, I would literally give it everything I had just like she did. And when I went home for the day, I'd leave it all behind. I could pick up in the morning right where I left off. And I would pick up better if I went home and recharged my battery.

So yeah, that elevator ride has stayed with me throughout my entire career. I've adopted that mentality 1000%. Whether I'm leading my team or doing solo projects, it's what I do. And it keeps me fresh. I give my all at work, but when it's over I basically shut it down. I mean, I outwork people half my age. And I will continue on this way for as long as I want to continue working. It keeps my energy levels where I want them to be, keeps me moving the way I want to move. And, in all honesty, though seemingly simple, it is one of the most valuable things I learned during my time in Washington.

Chapter Seventeen

A Policy and a Letter

Now what's also notable about this time is that I had access to arguably the best urban library in the country. You have to remember—this is 1997 or 1998. For all intents and purposes there is no Internet. No Google. There is no AI. There wasn't even Kindle. What you had were physical books, articles, and microfiche. If you don't know what microfiche was, look it up. It was cool. Part of me is sad that it's gone.

Anyway, HUD's library contained a tremendous amount of knowledge, all under one roof. I loved that place. During my lunch breaks, I would often eat really fast so I could go into the library and just peruse and read old first-edition policy documents. Like, the actual bills that were sent through Congress. I learned so much about urban development and public policy.

One day, I came across a document that was a real eye-opener. It stunned me to actually read those pages. They were from the Federal Housing Administration (FHA) of the mid-1930s. The part that intrigued me the most pertained to African Americans—specifically where it clearly expressed that no federal loans or insurance for home ownership or rental would be provided to African Americans. No support would be given to African Americans for housing. None. And we are talking about African Americans. Seventy years after the abolishment of slavery. We are talking Jim Crow. We are talking systemic governmentally-regulated racism at either its very finest—or its very worst—depending on one's point of view.

I found it appalling. It physically made me hurt to read this document that the United States Government supported. And I was reading the original. Yeah, it was wrapped in plastic like most of them were, but it was the original document. Original signatures. Original messed-up stuff.

I'd heard and studied all about "red lining," blockbusting, and the restrictions the federal government put on loans to African Americans to procure housing. I thought I knew everything there was about the subject. But, until I actually read that policy during that lunch hour, I realized I didn't know half of it. Reading that policy was like history coming alive for me. Reading that policy was human nature coming alive for me. Reading that policy made it so clear to me why my prayers to be saved from Park Chester never came true. Reading that policy gave me clarity in understanding the urban decay that had become the norm for so many African Americans—as well as the barriers to housing attainment and wealth creation for African Americans.

To this day, that lunch hour cemented in my mind a deep and unending desire to understand all of the challenges faced by poverty-stricken people in urban areas, particularly for African Americans. If I was ever going to overcome the barriers put in place by our government to thwart progress in affordable housing, I needed to understand them inside and out.

To see that document there, all that black ink on white paper, made the racial history of our country so obviously clear. It blew me away. And it was a truly enlightening experience.

As was this…

So, the President of the United States received a lot of mail. A ton of mail. More mail than any human being could respond to in any depth, even if his *only* job was to respond to mail. And back in the 90s, all of his mail came in envelopes with stamps. At one point in my time with HUD, my job was to read a portion of these letters and respond to them. I would read the letter, try to understand what the citizen wanted or needed, then, based upon my training and experience, I would think of a proper response and craft a letter.

After I was done with my letter I would pass it up a sort of chain of people who would approve what I wrote. There would be edits, things taken out, things added, etc. Once all was satisfactory, the letter would be given to President Bill Clinton so he could sign it.

I felt great honor to be tasked with this job.

One afternoon, a letter came in and I read it. I can't pretend to remember verbatim every single word, but a much-abridged version is something like this:

Hello Mr. President,

I live in a rural community and we have raised over $50,000 to accomplish a variety of community projects. We are very proud of the work that we are doing. We have built a community center and a neighborhood park. We wanted to write to you, Mr. President, to see what else we can do in order to continue to make our community great. Thank you.

Sincerely,
Sarah J. Robinson

I really liked the letter. The person who wrote it and the community in which they lived truly had done some great things. And they apparently believed in the wisdom of their government. I spent a long time thinking about my response before I began writing it out. I read the letter a few times. The humanity of it all was what really impressed me, what really moved me. And I wanted my response to be from a very human perspective. I wanted it to feel kind, and inspiring. And so, I started with "Dear Citizen" and started out by thanking her for taking the time to write the letter. I congratulated her on all they had done and wanted to still do to improve their community. I said how appreciative we were that they truly wanted to make their community great. I encouraged her to continue to put their heart and soul into their efforts. I wrote that we encourage you to work with others and to make sure that your community is a place of long-lasting livability.

Then, only after I felt like I had satisfied the human elements of the letter—how I felt that citizen would like to be responded to, how that citizen would like to be treated, did I proceed to outline a set of regulatory programs related to their inquiry that would be available to citizens looking for help in community improvement. I informed her how to apply for Community Development Block Grant Dollars, and so forth and so on down the line.

I was proud of my response. I felt like it would both satisfy and inspire the American citizen who wrote it—not to mention the up-striving community in which they lived.

I passed the letter up through the proper channels, up through the gauntlet of review, the chain of longstanding federal workers that every letter went through before being handed to the President.

When I saw what they had done, I was taken aback.

See, they'd taken out anything and everything related to the human-side of my letter. They took out everything that I thought a regular citizen would want to hear from the government, all the congratulatory praise, all the compassion, all the encouragement.

And they replaced it with something like this:

> According to regulation 24 CFR 570, the Community Development Block Grant Program is used to provide support for certain types of community redevelopment activities through your city, state, or country. We encourage you to have a conversation with your city to talk further about this option….

And that was to be handed to the President of the United States to be signed.

For me, it was a very disappointing response. Like reading the FHA policy toward African Americans and housing, this experience soured my experience in Washington. Like reading the government's urban renewal policies, better known as Negro Removal, in the communities destroyed by the policy it is a memory that I have not forgotten to this day. A memory I will never forget.

When I read the edited letter that the gauntlet of review sent out to those citizens, it helped me see why a lot of people in this country generally don't want to deal with the government—because of its insensitivity in communication, its insincerity of interaction, and its inability to work toward solving problems.

As a naïve individual who'd only been in Washington a short time, I just didn't understand it.

It's a major reason why I did not stay in the federal government after the program ended. I still have a lot of friends from the Fellowship who remained in the government. They have great careers. They have good hearts. They make changes when and how they can. But I just knew it wasn't for me. My path took me elsewhere.

Chapter Eighteen

The Complex

Let's go back for a little history about the apartment complex I keep talking about, the one called Park Chester. It was The Projects. It was the slum. It was bad, in all the ways.

And it's a great example of lack of investment in housing and the community when an area transitions from being all white to all black. When my mom, my brother, my sister, and I lived there, there hadn't been a single improvement made since back when it was apparently once a nice apartment complex full of white middle-class families. All I saw was the walls and ceilings looking like they'd cave in at any time. All I saw was trash everywhere. It was so rundown that I thought no one in their right mind would want to live there. We did. And it was not a very cool place.

Not at all.

In fact, it was *strange*. That's kind of the word I think of now when thinking back to then. *Strange* environment. *Strange* people. *Strange* life.

Imagine growing up and everything around you is just like cascading down in a cycle of bad to worse. The building was falling apart, crime was everywhere, drugs were everywhere, and being poor was in your face 24/7.

Park Chester may have been the worst of the worst. At one point, we were one of the only families still living there. We were in a four-plex building, and we were the only ones left still paying rent. To the left of us was an empty apartment. To the right of us was an empty apartment. Above us was an empty apartment. But, throughout those long nights of my youth, I'd constantly hear people in them. They'd get in, break in somewhere, rummage around to see what they could find. Get out of the rain in them. Squat in them for days on end. Do drugs in them for days on end. Scream and shout for days on end. Have sex in them, get in fights in them, tear themselves down in them. It was like being surrounded by zombies.

Shit went down outside the complex too.

One day I remember hiding in the bushes and watching a pretty aggressive shootout between the New Orleans Police Department and what looked like the Black Panthers. It was bad. It was violent. It was visceral, like being in a movie—except it was very, very real life.

I wondered why we were living in such a place. "Man," I thought so very often, "wouldn't it be great if someone would come rescue us."

I would just ask, "Why?" I asked that question all the time. "Why?… Why?"

I never got a good answer. All I got was about the biggest, earliest crucible of my life. All I got was learning how to survive. All I got was that I didn't want this for my future. If I ever had kids, I knew they wouldn't grow up in such a place surrounded by such terrible things.

Years later as an adult, I was speaking to a professor at Columbia University, and I was able to connect some dots. A PhD candidate wrote her dissertation on this apartment complex, documenting the various failures of Park Chester.

And I'll tell you what, the origins of what I do for a living—working to provide human beings with safe, healthy, affordable places to live—are rooted in my childhood. The reason I do what I do is because we were forced to move around so much, evicted so much, put on the out and out so much with no other choice.

Living at the Park Chester Apartments, I truly believe, is why I do what I do. May you and your loved ones never have to experience the squalor, the chaos, the terror of a place like that. It was a fucking nightmare.

Chapter Nineteen
A New Challenge

I n 1996-1997, near the end of my time as a Presidential Management Fellow in D.C., I had an opportunity to partner up with a colleague friend of mine. Her name was Dr. Susan Leland, and she was doing some great work in public policy and public administration. I knew Dr. Leland from Minnesota State University where we both completed our master's degree in public administration. We teamed up to write a proposal for a conference in Philadelphia. Even at my relatively young age, I suppose my work impressed her. "Wow, Eric," she told me. "You can go as far as you want in this field. But to go that far, you should go on and get your PhD."

"Me?"

"I really think you should."

I was honest with her. "I wouldn't even know where to begin."

"How about this. While you're in Philadelphia for the conference, schedule some time to go and visit the University of Delaware. Their program is highly-ranked in public policy and urban affairs. It would be a good opportunity for you to see what the program is all about."

Her vote of confidence gave me the confidence I needed, and opened up a new doorway of possibility in my life. But, I mean, as much as I loved education—as much as I loved learning everything I possibly could—a PhD had never really been on my radar. I remembered a stat that something like only .03% of African American males had a doctorate.

It seemed daunting to say the least.

But Susan's belief in me got me really intrigued, so I set up a visit to the university. I got on campus and went from office to office, meeting with different professors; we're getting into dynamic conversations of 20-30 minutes, and I can't believe all the time they gave me. I mostly just listen to them, trying to absorb what I can. I started getting that "in awe" feeling again. I'm in awe of their knowledge. I'm in awe of their wisdom. But they're also making sure to tell me about the rigors of the program. A lot of their words almost felt like a warning *not* to apply. They were like, "Hey, Eric, it really is a ton of work." But the more these professors talked, the harder they made the journey seem, the more I started wanting it.

Being on that campus and talking to these professors was like being at an all-star game of public policy. Two of the faculty members I met during my visit were Dr. Margeret Wilder and Dr. Bob Denhardt. These were world-renowned scholars, clear front-runners in the field. They were two of my heroes. And I was like, *If I get accepted here, I can learn from them?* The more time I spent on campus, the more I started to feel like I belonged there. The program combined both practice and theory. I already had a strong background in practical work from my time at the Fellowship, but getting this PhD seemed like it would complete my training in the theoretical side—build up my skill set to a truly well-rounded place.

I had one more meeting before my visit was over. I walked into this professor's office and I remember just looking up at all the books on the shelves; old books, new books, hundreds of 'em. Research papers were stacked on the floor, and there were just pages everywhere. The smell of paper was palpable, and it felt like knowledge was everywhere. I shook my head, just having a hard time believing someone could read all this material. "Wow," I say inwardly. "This is serious stuff—and these people are truly living this life."

The program just felt like home. Earning my PhD felt like a calling. While I also toured American University and George Washington among a few others, nothing felt quite as perfect of a fit as the University of Delaware. Yeah, it would be a long road. Yeah, it would take years of my life. But wow, what a huge accomplishment it would be.

I needed a new challenge, and this felt like it.

Chapter Twenty

In Deep

When I started the application process for the University of Delaware, I knew I was no shoo-in. I buckled down and gave my all in the process. When I submitted it, I had to wait. And then wait some more. Finally, I got the acceptance letter in the mail.

It felt like a gift.

But it was a gift that I would really, truly have to earn. Plus, because of the time of year I'd applied, I had nearly a full year before my classes would start up. Though my Presidential Fellowship had ended, I was still working for HUD as a full-time policy analyst to pay the bills. I was living down in Silver Springs, Maryland, and five days a week I would ride the subway to get to work, catching the same Red Line Metro to Seventh and D Street in downtown D.C. There were other commuters who were on the train with me every day as well. You started to get to recognize them. And one man stood out to me beyond the others. Why is that? Well, for the entire duration of the ride, this guy would read. He wasn't reading magazines or the newspaper. He would read books. Thick ones. He'd just devour them, a new book every three days or so. But what amazed me the most was this: the guy was blind. Every morning, I would watch him read books in braille, his fingers moving left to right and down the page, page-after-page. And he had this flat-out locked-in focus about him. I would sit in awe and watch him go, thinking, *Man, this guy has one of the ultimate disabilities, but without fail he reads like a scholar every single morning. How much does this guy learn even before he goes into work?*

His laser focus just sort of osmosed on me. It got to me. It challenged me. I knew I needed to raise my game in order to get prepared for the journey of my PhD trek. "If this man can read like this without the gift of sight," I told myself. "Then I can too. No excuses."

Borrowing from the leadership I found in my blind friend on the metro, I started reading throughout my commutes on the Red Line Metro too. I was at the library and the bookstore all the time, just picking up anything I could on public affairs and public policy. I read them on the train to and from HUD. I read them in the park at lunch, and I read them on the couch at night. I mean, during those months of preparing to become a PhD candidate, I read every major book in my field.

And, when classes finally started up, I knew it had given me the edge I needed; even though I moved up to Newark, Delaware to be closer to campus, I had to keep working full-time at HUD to pay the bills—plus, I'd taken on a 20-hour per week research fellowship. In short, I was about to be really, really busy. And had that blind friend of mine not taught me how to see the light of what I needed to see, I would not have been able to embark upon what I needed to do. I thank that man every day. For, with his leadership-by-example, I was able to do something quite rare in a PhD student: before my program even began, I was able to define what my dissertation topic was going to be.

The dissertation is pretty important for a PhD candidate—and a high percentage of students have a difficult time even defining exactly what it is they want to complete, let alone researching and writing it out to a passable level. Not me. My topic, expanded and honed by all my pre-coursework reading, was going build off my practical work during my fellowship and at HUD; I was going to focus on the whys, hows, ins, outs, ups, downs, and all-arounds of the continuous election of black mayors in majority-black cities. The primary question I would explore was: to what extent does the expenditure of the most flexible federal dollars—the Community Development Block Grant Program—affect these black mayors being so continuously elected. And I would need to write about 300 pages to answer it sufficiently.

But we'll get to the dissertation later. For now, let's start with the first day of classes.

I entered the program armed with what I felt like was great momentum. "I'm going to fly through this thing," I told myself.

After the first day, though, reality hit me like a sledgehammer. A really big sledgehammer. Walking off campus that day, it hit home hard. "Yeah," I muttered to myself. "This PhD is going to take a full five years. Half a decade, here we go."

Still confident, I buckled down even harder. I was determined to succeed. Time passed, and we got to the first exams. Yep, very tough. Quite difficult. When I got my score back, I just looked at my grade on the paper and I was blank-faced and devastated. "Wait a minute," I said inwardly. "Maybe I'm not as good as I think I am?"

But I took the lesson to heart. I drilled down even more. I had to focus. And with my full-time job and my research fellowship (and my commute), I'll tell you this: I had to *balance*. I started waking up at four o'clock in the morning. And I went back to relying on that little boy growing up in New Orleans that was still inside of me. Back to being Captain America with the garbage can lid against the older thugs. Back to proving to my family and the streets that they couldn't hold me down. Back to writing out my basketball goals in high school. I reached inside and asked that young boy for strength—and I started attacking this PhD with an academic fervor I hadn't yet known was possible.

I converted one of the bedrooms in my apartment to an office. I kept all my school-related materials in there. That was my battleground. I would walk in there, set a clock for four, six, nine hours—and not leave, not do anything but study and learn for whatever timeframe I set for myself. Nothing academic would ever leave that room. Not a book, not an article. I compartmentalize my life. It helped me stay sane, helped me fall asleep quickly and somehow wake up refreshed a few hours later. I would accomplish what I wanted to accomplish for a day. Never less. And I did that day after day.

In time, those days added up. And it really accelerated my work. My capacity for reading grew. My capacity for thinking grew. My capacity to "go beyond" grew. I was totally honed in. And because I was totally honed in, I truly started getting the most out of the program. The classes and the faculty were just outstanding. I remember one specific professor, Dr. Tamara Haraven. She was a very strong teacher, a great professor and highly respected around campus. She was a prisoner of war during World War II, and she was tough. Some students were literally terrified to take her class but I made sure to get in there. She really just tested your ability, and I remember thanking her for both the demanding work she gave us and the pressure she put on us. She was an outstanding scholar, a top-level mind—and she had a big heart.

She once told our class something that I hold onto to this day: "In this class, your opinions do not matter. When you come into this classroom, you better be able to back up everything you say with some sort of reference that is based on some sort of logical framework."

Wow! *My opinions didn't matter?!* Those words made me think differently. Those words made me look at things differently. Those words turned me on to the absolute necessity of logic and of backing my views up with fact.

Those words still stick with me today, in every job I do.

I'm zoned in, locked in, grooving like Dr. J on the basketball court. I'm an academic, and I'm in my element. I'm answering my call—and therefore I am home.

More time passes, and I'm preparing for my qualifying exams. These things are tough. These things are long, and these things are grueling. These things are a separator. These things test you on everything and more.

And they're timed.

To pass the qualifying exams, one has to know their stuff inside and out, backwards and forwards—and be thinking and writing as fast as The Flash can run a marathon.

My cohort and I have become close. The seven of us respect the heck out of each other. We know that not all of us will pass. We wish each other luck and go our separate ways.

I remember picking up my exam in its sealed packet. It is thick and foreboding. "Eric," I am told, "you have 48 hours to complete this exam and return it—or else it will not be considered, and you will fail."

I look at the clock on the wall, and the minute hand already seems to be moving at the speed of the second hand. I literally run to my car, speed home, take a sip of water, go into my office, put on a mix of Beethoven and Bach, stop blinking, and get to work.

The clock continues to turn. I think and I write. Think and write. Think and write. Scarf some food. Think and write. Think and write. Take a nap. Think and write. Think and write.

Taking that exam was the fastest passage of time I'd ever experienced in my life. But I turned in my qualifying exam with minutes to spare.

The term was over.

I waited all through June just biting my fingernails and checking the mailbox to see if I passed—to see if I have to go backward and redo the last semester, or if I get to move forward.

I get to know the mailman.

It's mid-July, and I was still waiting to see the trajectory of my life.

I wait some more, my fingernails short and my mind racing.

And, then, one afternoon in late July, right before the next term commences, an envelope arrived.

I ran inside, my breath heavy and my heart racing as I tore the thing open.

The first line does not begin, "We regret to inform you…" No, that first word is one of the greatest words in the English language: "Congratulations…"

I'd done it.

The feeling was nothing short of spectacular.

I passed my qualifying exam.

And I'm the only one of my cohorts who did it on the first try.

Chapter Twenty-One

Family Beatdowns

As a boy, I got to go to a summer camp one summer. It was called Camp Abbey in Covington, Louisiana. The camp was cool, truly a "go out into the woods and sleep in your tent-cabins and do all the outdoor things" type of place. It seemed idyllic, a kid from the streets getting to go out and play at the lake and among the trees.

The experience was provided through Holy Ghost Catholic Church, and I was so excited to go. It was about the only slice of true Americana I think I got as a kid. It was like *Dirty Dancing*. It was like the place where all the white kids got to go. But, yeah, it was also a little bit like the summer camp in *Friday the 13th* where Jason goes and does his thing. I mean, no one died, but there was a little bit of horror to it too.

See, near the end of the summer there was this competition called The Golden Knight. It consisted of a series of competitions: swimming, diving, canoeing, and archery. If you won it, you got the Golden Knight Award. It was all I wanted, man. I wanted to win that award more than I'd ever wanted anything.

But they only gave out one award. No matter all the different ages at the camp, there was only one winner. I was 13, and not many boys younger than me had ever won, much less even really competed.

Still, regardless of your age, you could enter. So, I did. I wanted this thing bad. I trained hard all summer and put my hat in the ring. My brother did too. All the best athletes did.

Competition day came.

I went out and did my thing.

Against all the older kids, against all the odds, I won.

I was so proud. So absolutely joyful. It felt like I was walking on water.

After I got my medal, I walked up to my brother in hopes to get his congratulations, get his praise. I walked up to him and he just looked at me with a steel glare. "You should have let me win," he said.

"What?"

"I'm the oldest, you should have let me win." And he walked off.

No hug. No high five. No praise. Nothin'.

C'mon man.

My whole life it seemed like he was trying to beat me down. Like he didn't want me to succeed. Like he didn't want me to do my thing. So often, I felt like my mom was the same way. Like when she'd wake me up in the night and beat me up for forgetting to do the dishes or putting hot tabasco sauce in my mouth for saying a bad word. Stuff like that. And don't get me started on the spankings; they were so bad that I'd scream out for help, hoping someone would come and save me.

My mom would also do odd things to make me feel less than—for example, forcing me to wear two left-footed football cleats.

We used to watch a lot of football games, and we loved the sport. We all wanted to be O.J. Simpson, who often ran through the snow while playing for the Buffalo Bills. In New Orleans, of course, it rarely snowed. But one Christmas in the mid-70s it did! It snowed. And we also received New Orleans Saints football uniforms. Man, I was pumped to go outside and run in the snow like O.J.—especially when I opened a present which contained football cleats.

But, like I said, they were both left-footed shoes. I went to my mom and told her I had two left cleats.

"Well," she said, "you better wear them because I am not taking them back."

I was devastated. But despite the awkwardness and pain, I proceeded to put on my two left cleats and went out and ran in the snow with the ball under my arm like I was O.J.

My feet hurt a lot after that, and nothing was ever said to me again about the two left cleats.

Another time was when I was in high school and my mom didn't want me to go on the senior trip. I mean, I truly felt like I'd earned it. I was an all-star student and captain of the basketball team. I participated in the homecoming court and even square danced on behalf of the school in competitions. I was presented with an award my senior year naming me the Gentleman of the Year. But at the end of the year, when all the seniors were going to get on a bus to Disney World and have a night in the park with other seniors across the South, she didn't want me to go. It was all I wanted. I mean, they closed down the park and for the entire night it was just seniors in high school getting to go have fun. It wasn't expensive at all. I believe it cost $75 dollars to attend.

She didn't want me to go.

It was weird.

Word got out that I wasn't going. The principal of the school got word of it. "Why isn't Eric going?" he asked around.

"His mom doesn't want to pay for it."

The principal didn't like that. He felt like I deserved to go. It bugged him so much that one afternoon he came out to my house.

My mom and I answered the door. We talked a bit about me going, and my mom's not having any of it. Then he just said, "The school will pay for it," and he turned around and walked away.

At least my principal had my back.

See, my mom and I had a weird relationship. She'd always tell me, "You're angry. You have an anger problem."

I wasn't angry. Heck, maybe I was, but to me, inside, internally, to the boy I was, I wasn't angry—I was just resisting. I sensed I was being demeaned and treated as undeserving. I saw my surroundings. I saw my situation. Lots of things just did not make sense. And I didn't like it, and I didn't want to go along with it. I resisted. I disrupted the status quo, I did not accept it.

I knew I could not be complacent. I knew there was more. I knew there was "better" out there. I wasn't angry, I just wanted a fair shot. I wanted to be treated with respect and dignity at home and throughout the streets of New Orleans.

Chapter Twenty-Two

Endlessness

The next PhD semester was all about the dissertation. I'd passed the qualifying exams, and the next (last, and greatest) hurdle was the dissertation.

Doctorate school is mostly about oral defenses and writing papers. That term, regardless of the class, I found a way to make every single paper I wrote somehow linked to the topic of my dissertation. Sometimes I had to get creative to do that, but I didn't want any dead weight. I wanted everything to move forward in a seamless, efficient manner. I tied everything together so I would not be wasting my time researching areas that had nothing to do with that ultimate paper. Like I had before, I set my goals, and knew it would pay off.

The cities I focused on were New Orleans, Detroit, Atlanta, and Washington D.C. These four predominantly black cities fit my criteria for consistent elections of black mayors. I collected data, researching any books and articles I could; I went out and visited these cities multiple times, really trying to get to know them. I was preparing the early work for the dissertation. This was important, because to truly begin the writing process, a PhD candidate has to have a "concept draft" approved by their committee. This was another hurdle, another reason why I was so thankful for that blind man back on the subway; I was prepared for it, and more than a few others in my situation weren't. Not nearly everyone gets approval of their "concept draft." This means they basically have to alter, if not start anew, on their project.

My committee was tough. It was Dr. Tamara Hareven, whom I've mentioned, along with top professors Dr. Bob Warner and Dr. Margaret Wilder. All three of them were elite in the field, their body of work off the charts. All three of them have eagle eyes and are tough as nails.

I worked my rear-end off and finally finished my concept draft. I submitted it to my committee so they can read and critique it, discuss it among themselves, and prepare to question me on it—to see if it, and I, have the muster.

A short time after I dropped it off, they've read it and they're ready for me to defend it. And I'm ready for another huge hurdle in the marathon-long PhD-sprint.

The time and date are set.

I walked into the School of Urban Affairs and Public Policy. I ascended the stairs to the iconic second-floor conference room, the one right next to the Center for Community Development. It felt like I was walking in quicksand, but I kept on going. I knocked on the door.

"Come in."

I entered, and all my committee members were sitting sternly around a large round table. Like something out of Arthurian Legend, the air in the room was heavy. Man, was I nervous. The time had come to walk the plank and defend my dissertation.

There was no small-talk as they went straight into the business at hand. They asked questions. I answered. They spoke to what they believed were the strengths of my arguments, the weaknesses too. They pointed out more flaws than I wanted them to. More questions. I try to breathe as I answer as best, as succinctly, as I can.

After what felt like an eternity, they told me, "Eric, you are excused for the time being. You can stand outside while we discuss what you have presented."

I walked out of the room still nervous as heck but knowing I gave it my best shot. I'd just gone toe-to-toe with three of the top minds in my field. I don't know how they will judge me and my work. I walk the hallway, just pacing back and forth and biting my fingernails. I feel my mind racing in zig-zagging circles. It was one of the hardest things I'd ever done, being outside in the hallway while they debated my future. I felt so alone, like I'd put in so much work—written 300+ pages, researched the topic for nearly five years—and now it felt like it was all out of my control.

I bite my fingernails some more. Pace back and forth while constantly checking my watch. Forty-five minutes tick by at a snail's pace. Finally, the door opens. "Come on in Eric," I hear. "We want to talk to you."

My stomach is in knots. I walk in and take another frightful seat at the round table.

There is a silence, then, "Eric, you have laid out fine arguments."

"And…?"

"And we accept your topic and your arguments. We have made our comments for you to improve upon. But you are approved to move forward with finalizing your dissertation so you may earn your PhD."

I can't believe it.

But then again, I can. We all shake hands, and I walk away from the round table and out of the conference room. I begin immediately reflecting back to my early days in New Orleans. I think of all my friends who never got such an opportunity, all my friends who ended up in jail or dead. I think of all the naysayers who did not believe or support me. *Man, I just got my dissertation approved! All I have to do now is refine it, tighten it up a bit,* I think to myself. I walk down the hallway, down the stairs and out the door into the outside air. At that moment, I felt like it was all worth it, all the sacrifice, everything going back to the blind leader on the subway.

I go right back to my home office, start with the refining, the completion. A few weeks later, I submitted the final draft. It is now 2003— and the journey that I started back in 1997 is nearing the mountaintop.

I turned everything in.

In short order, everything gets approved. "Congratulations," I hear all around, "we will see you at graduation…"

But, still, it doesn't feel real.

I must have called the office four or five times asking, "Is this for sure? Like, is there anything else you need…?"

It got to the point where the office was almost chuckling as they'd tell me, "Yes, Eric. You are good. Everything is completed."

I'd done it. I'd completed the incompletable journey. It felt like I could fly!

I still have a nightmare, a recurring nightmare, where the school office calls me up and starts out with, "Yeah, we're terribly sorry, Eric— but you still need to come back and complete your dissertation."

"Why?!" I ask.

"Oh, you didn't do this, this, or that...."

But then I awake from that nightmare. I awake back to my reality, the reality where I'm a black man with a PhD.

PhD. Postscript:

There was a truck stop on I-95 South. I used to stop there three or four times a week as I drove to and from Delaware to Washington to work my full-time HUD job and get my research fellowship done. It was kind of a midway-point marker, and I used it to break up the drive and get a study session in. I would walk to the back of the truck stop to my favorite seat at my favorite table, get out a book or my computer, and get my work done.

I came to be there so much that some of the truckers started recognizing me. They'd come up to me, hand outstretched. "Hey, man, I see you here all the time—what route do you drive?"

I'd shake their hand, look them in the eye. "Thanks for saying hi. But I'm not a trucker. I'm a PhD student up in Delaware."

They were good people, and some would raise an eyebrow and ask a follow-up question or two. Some would just look at me funny, like I was lying to them or something. Then they'd walk off and get back to their route.

And I'd buckle down into my books and get back on mine.

The only thing I really wish had gone different about my PhD journey was something about my graduation. I called up my mom, told her I'd made it. I invited her up to attend the ceremony. I told her I'd pay for the flight and the hotel. I told her I'd buy her some new clothes if she wanted.

"Nope," she says through the line. "I'm not coming up."

It hurt. Can't say that it didn't. I guess it was still part of the undeserving attitude toward me. At any rate, who knows.

My brother and sister never even called me up to say congratulations. That stung too, can't say that it didn't.

At least my aunt and uncle showed up to celebrate with me, to be there with me. That was nice of them. And I will always appreciate them for that…

Chapter Twenty-Three

Hurt

Like I've said, I loved my comic books. By the time I was 14, I'd collected a bunch of them. I got some given to me, and any spare change I could get I'd buy whatever I could. I had 'em all. Two-thousand of them. I kept them in a box in the corner of my room. It was a real source of pride and inspiration for me.

By the time we were moving again, it got to where I had quite the collection.

We packed up all our things. I boxed up all my things, heck there wasn't much to pack up, but I made sure to box up my comics real nice. I taped it shut. Put the box where I was supposed to put it.

We make the move like we'd done a dozen times and get to the new place and start unpacking.

I look right away for my box of comics. Can't find them. I look some more, look all over.

"Mom!" I called out. "Where's my box of comic books?"

She didn't give much of an answer.

I looked and looked and looked. But that box was nowhere to be found. My comics were nowhere to be found. The longer I looked, the more I knew they didn't make the move with us. The more I looked, I knew my heroes were no longer with me.

I mean, I'd boxed them up real nice. I'd put the work in, put them where right where they were supposed to go.

But they didn't make the trip with us. Didn't make the trip for me. Worst of all, it felt intentional. I think my mom didn't see how important they were to me. No, I knew she didn't see how important they were to me. Maybe she thought they were dumb. Maybe she didn't like me idolizing all them white heroes. Maybe she didn't believe in the power of myth and story. I don't know.

All I know is that it didn't seem like my mom felt they weren't worth the space, worth the effort to move one more box.

It hurt a lot, and I cried a lot that night.

I cried because it was sad not to have my comics to read, to not have my comics to escape to. But what hurt maybe even more was that it felt like I had these forces in my life going against me. Like, those books were so vital for me to get through. And no one in my family saw that? My one little slice of happiness wasn't worth one more box?

Hey, maybe comic books are silly. Maybe baseball cards are silly. Maybe stuffed animals are silly. But my comic books weren't silly to me.

They were very, very necessary.

And when my box of comic books didn't make that move with me that night, what I internalized was that my mom didn't think I was going to be much in my life. Yeah, it felt like a slight. Yeah, it felt like an F You.

Yeah, it hurt. Man, just thinking about that night still hurts. It hurts because I think back to that little boy that was me.

I know we're supposed to move on. I know we're supposed to work through all our childhood stuff. I know I've told you about getting into fights and about seeing people murdered in front of my eyes. But having my comic books ripped away from me—my male role models ripped away from me—that really f-ing hurt.

Chapter Twenty-Four

On Rappers and Representatives

My professional journey was built upon the notion that I had a lot of catching up to do. It goes back to how I grew up— and to reading *Countering the Conspiracy to Destroy Black Boys*. Those two things have always kept me moving, kept me trying to catch up so one day I can finally get ahead. I feel like I'm there now, but for a long time it was like a basketball game. Just go, go, go. I mean, from pretty early on I had this notion that working one job for 30 years was never going to do it for me. Even getting the PhD—a lot of people told me not to do it, told me that I was making good money and doing good things without it. But I wanted that degree, wanted to keep going because I knew it would help me do truly creative, dynamic, and disruptive things—the only things that make actual change.

They say that life is not a race. But with how I grew up and with the color of my skin, I knew I needed to keep moving or else I wouldn't get to where I wanted to go. I never saw the traditional playbook as a viable option. And that has made all the difference.

I signed on to a two-year appointment for the Louisiana Department of Economic Development—back to the home state, back to my roots. My job was to secure funding for the competitive grants for the great state of the Bayou. People told me I was doing good work. The main reason I felt this was so, was because I successfully made one simple point over and over again. After so much repetition, I suppose people could no longer turn a deaf ear.

The simple point I made was this: Louisiana is ranked dead last in competitive grants. That's how I got the Louisiana government to support the idea of a "grants matching fund." That's how I was able to generate a great deal of money for a great deal of important economic improvement projects.

Some groups of people took note.

One group was the United States Congress.

That's why they invited me to come out and speak in front of the House Ways and Means Committee.

I traveled out to D.C. to do my thing and they put me up in about the nicest hotel room I'd ever been in. This thing was plush, nice, and only about two blocks from Union Station.

And I have to tell you this: even though this story comes at the outset of this professional journey section, I was still in the midst of the last daunting days of my PhD program at the time. That's why I showed up with a bookbag full of books. That's why—though I should have been over-the-moon with excitement at speaking in front of Congress—I was down and out.

Because I was tired.

I was exhausted.

I was feeling like I had nothing left to give.

In truth, I was all but resigned to giving up on the PhD dream. With the full-time work, that research fellowship, and working on getting that dissertation approved, it was proving too much for me.

Yeah, I was honored to be asked to go before Congress to present some of the dynamic things I'd been doing in Louisiana, but I was kind of burnt out on life. The dissertation was simply taking its toll, taking so much of me, taking forever and a day. The light at the end of the tunnel was dim at best, barely visible most of the time. I was questioning things. I mean, if I was being asked to go to Washington to speak in front of the House Ways and Means, did I really need to get that dang piece of paper?

In short, I was feeling sorry for myself. Despite all that shit in childhood, that's not a feeling I'd had too often in my life. I couldn't think. I couldn't prep for the Congress thing or get any positive work done on my dissertation.

So, I put on some sneakers and went for a walk. I walked out of my room, down through the lobby and into the outside air. I walked over to Union Station and was just ambling about, taking in the sights and killing time. Almost unconsciously, I walked into Tower Records and started browsing the CDs. Like I usually do, I gravitated toward the hip hop section. As a younger kid, I wanted to be a DJ (even got an FCC license to be on the radio), and I was a huge fan of Hip Hop music and its origins. As I made it to the Hip Hop section in Tower Records, I picked up a few cases, flipped them over to look at the titles, and put them back down.

Then one really caught my eye—Eric B and Rakim. These are my boys. I mean, they're one of the best rap composers of all time and I'm holding their greatest hits album. I can't believe I don't already own it,

131

so I walk up to the cashier and buy it on the spot. I'm done idling, I want to get back to my hotel room and put on the CD. At this moment in my life, I know what I need is music—good, sweet music.

I walk back up through the lobby to my room, put my keycard in the door, walk in and start playing the CD. And I'll tell you what, right from the get-go, these songs started giving me what I needed. The first track played right into the second. I started feeling it. I got so charged that I'm stompin' around the room and hollering out. I'm getting pumped. I'm getting my groove back. I stopped feeling sorry for myself—and that night I wrote 30 pages for my dissertation and prepared for my meeting in the morning before the Congress of the United States of America.

God bless Eric B and Rakim.

I wake up the next day ready to go. Sure, I have some butterflies in my stomach but I feel prepared. I feel balanced. I feel like myself.

I make my way over to the Rayburn Building where a lot of the Representatives are located. I go in and meet a few of them, shake some hands, do the small talk, but I focus my time with Congressman William Jefferson of Louisiana. I can't believe he knows me by name. I'm in that place of awe again. It's just amazing that this is real.

Eventually, I make my way into the Congressional building. Down into the chamber. I walk in with wide eyes and try my best to humbly take that seat you've seen on TV, in front and below the heralded congresspeople. I'm set to speak with two mayors, the Mayor of Memphis and one other whose city now eludes me. I look around and I catch myself with my jaw agape, again so in awe that I am right here right now.

The proceedings begin. I sit up as straight as I can in my seat. Those butterflies are still there, but I use my experience to push them aside. When my turn comes to speak, I just go for it. I speak from the heart. I lay out how I devised putting the different chess pieces together in order to get the checkmate answer for those matching grants. As I speak, I see (and almost feel) the congressional members perking up, looking in. When I started speaking, they were leaning back in their chairs, holding side conversations—but now I felt a rapt audience.

And so, I dug in deeper. Their eyes looking right at mine, I speak on and they ask me follow-up question after follow-up question. Their heads nod. They're digging what I'm saying, and I know it.

I went into the hearing thinking that the two mayors were going to speak the bulk of the time, but it turned out the opposite. I'd say 80% or more of the questions were directed at me.

"How did you come up with these different strategies?"

"Why did you choose to do this work, Eric?"

"What kind of advice can you impart to others who want to pursue such a path…?"

After a while, I felt kind of embarrassed, like I was getting way too much airtime. "With all due respect," I said, "these two mayors of major cities undoubtedly know more than me—maybe you should talk to them…?"

Eventually, the conversation turned away from me and rightfully toward the mayors. After that, I was finally able to draw a breath. I looked around the room. You could feel the history. You could feel the gravitas. You could feel Lincoln. You could feel Washington and Jefferson and JFK. It was surreal. I felt so in awe but also so very in the moment.

After everything was over and done, a couple of the congressmen came up to me and were like, "Hey, Mr. Johnson, come on and talk with us a little more…"

And all of a sudden, I found myself in the side-rooms of Congress, just chumming it up with all these Representatives. They were engaging, continuing to ask me questions and actually listening to my answers.

It was so cool.

When I finally left, my chest was all pumped out, feeling good. Had I not picked up that Eric B and Rakim CD the night before, I'm not sure I'd have been ready for it…

Chapter Twenty-Five

A Pitch and a Success

After I officially graduated with my PhD, I was hired to work down in Pompano Beach, Florida as their Director of Regional Housing. I liked the area, the people, and the work. One of the most dynamic things I got to spearhead was launching a local microenterprise incubation-program that would provide training for low-income individuals to create businesses for themselves. To get it going, I led an effort to secure $300,000 from the community redevelopment agency.

The problem was that, in order to do so, we needed to create a loan fund. To get the loan fund going, I needed to take a gamble and make a play with the local banking community.

I really wanted this loan fund to go through. I mean, I really believed in all the good that this microenterprise program would do for the community. It would give low-income people an economic leg up and a boost of pride. It would help lift up a lot of people and, in doing so, help lift up the entire community. I reached out to 12-15 bankers in the community reinvestment space, and reserved a plush banquet room in one of the area's nicest hotels. We laid everything out first class—the setting, the table, the chairs, the food, the podium. Though this was really a novel concept and we hadn't pulled anything like this off before, we wanted to make it at least look like we knew what we were doing.

After introductions, I walked up to the podium and gave my pitch. I spoke on "the importance of inclusion"—of including the low-income people in the community on the work that would be done on the big redevelopment projects that were about to be undertaken. I argued that instead of hiring outside contractors (and essentially then fighting the community by leaving them out of the money) why couldn't we create a loan-fund microenterprise incubation that would allow citizens to participate? That would allow citizens to be part of the rebuild? That would keep the money local? I spoke of how it would be a win-win for the community. I spoke of how it would reduce conflict within the community while at the same time creating wealth. It was a symbiotic system. The audience picked up what I was putting down, and I could feel the energy in the room.

The banks were particularly interested in what I was proposing because they came from the community reinvestment portion of the bank. This meant that they were required by the federal government to invest such-and-such a proportion of their funds into projects like this. So, in some sense, it was really an opportunity that we were teeing up for them. We showed them how they could meet their requirements for the federal government while at the same time doing truly great work for the community.

The pitch went great, and a week or two later the calls started coming in.

"Hello," I'd answer.

And the responses were like, "Yes, Dr. Johnson, we want to participate in the loan fund," and, "Yes, we actually want to get a seat on the finance committee to ensure that we are doing things properly."

"Sounds good," I'd say. And I'd hang up the phone with a satisfied smile. I knew how much good this was going to do.

Once it got going, that microenterprise program in Pompano Beach really became a model for how to get similar actions done. The fund launched, the local businesses got going, the work got done, and local low-income people were able to make money while helping rebuild their community. Plus—and this is a big one—the repayment rate hovered around 98%. The stereotype is that low-income people don't pay back their loans. (That's why it's so often so difficult for that population to get a loan). But this program proved the stereotype wrong in a big way.

It was never about how low-income people from the community don't pay their loans back—it actually proved the opposite. When given the loan, 98% of the people that received a loan were making their payments on time. With only a 2% default rate, that's about as good as it gets anywhere.

The whole community came together, and it was one huge success. Because it was such a success, it came to be studied—and followed. Both the idea and the process by which we got things done on that project has become a template that has been followed time and again. I'm really proud of that. I'm really proud of all the work we did back then to help out a lot of folks. Low-income people were able to create their own businesses. And those businesses were able to help rebuild a community. It was so obvious, it's just that it had never really been done before. We had to pave the way—and that work we did has helped a lot of other individuals and a lot of other communities since.

Why?

Because symbiotic, people-first, win-win scenarios are a good thing.

Chapter Twenty-Six

The Other Side of Canal

Growing up, a lot of my male family members got decimated by the drug trade and crack epidemic. It was everywhere. And it was definitely in my family and in our circle of people. So many of the men I knew got caught up in it. It was like wildfire. And yeah, it decimated my family. Call it what you want, but that was a hard time if you were a black man in an urban area. That's the truth.

And when you start getting into drugs, you get addicted, to both using and selling. To fund your addiction, you have to have money. If you don't have any education and no marketable skills and you need money, you do some pretty dumb things. I saw it all. Robbing. Killing. Gangs. Death Row cases. High profile murders. Heck, close male family members, who I miss dearly, were murdered or ended up in jail. In several cases, they made the "breaking news" on TV.

It was heavy. It was real—so real it almost seemed fake sometimes, like a movie or something. I mean, though the film was based out in the West Coast, when *Boyz n the Hood* came out a decade or so later, I was like, "Wow, my childhood was not too dissimilar." Black-on-black violence. Drugs. Shit going down. That was life.

The role that Ice Cube played was like one of my younger cousins. He was a big deal. A known dude. Why? Because he was one of the hardest motherfuckers around.

And me, as I got into my teen years, I was kind of like the football player in that movie, Rickey. Rickey got a little bit of a pass from the drugs and the gang-banging because his community, his *people*, wanted him to get out. Deep down they wanted Rickey to get that scholarship, to get out into the word and do some things.

I got a bit of a pass too because I was a good basketball player and a good student. I was clean cut and it was known that I didn't drink or smoke. I was the guy that if I was put in a room full of drugs, I'd make some sort of excuse. "You know I forgot my wallet in the car," I'd say. "I gotta go get it." And I'd be out. And no one gave me that much shit about it. They knew I wasn't going to be in that room, and all was good. I could go into the hardest housing projects, be around the hardest gangsters and thugs, and it was like, "Oh, that's Big E. He's not gonna do this stuff so don't even waste your time."

That was my rep.

But in New Orleans, you have to understand there were borderlands. There were boundaries. Ours was Canal Street. You cross Canal Street, that's unknown territory. There ain't no reps beyond Canal Street. No one knew me as "Big E" beyond Canal Street. I was told from an early age, "Don't ever cross Canal Street. That's the unknown."

That was a rule. Because you go over there, people don't know you. You don't got no friends. You don't got no protection. You're out in the woods with the wolves.

So, it was known not to cross Canal Street. But then I got a girlfriend who lived over there, so one day I had to test the maxim. I crossed the line of demarcation and right away found myself in unfamiliar territory. Every guy I passed was looking at me like, "Man, you're not from around here—you don't belong around here."

But I had to see my girlfriend, right?

One thing I did that was really stupid, was that to impress her I had put on a pair of brand-new Dr. J sneakers. These things were hot at the time, like gold out here—and they put even more of a target on my back because if someone beat me up good enough they could take my shoes as a prize. I walked on fast, fearful steps toward my girlfriend's house.

I made it inside.

We hung out for a couple hours and then she walked me to the front door to give me a kiss and say goodbye.

But outside was trouble. Not one, not two, not three, but five guys just mean mugging me. To get back to my side of town I'd have to walk right past them. They were some of the same guys I'd seen on my way in—they'd followed me and had nothing better to do than to wait for me to leave.

I didn't like the look of it, and neither did my girlfriend. "How about you come back inside, Eric. Wait for them to leave?"

I was like, yeah, I'd rather spend more time with my girl than deal with these five thugs. We go back inside and periodically look out the window. The guys aren't dispersing, and they're looking meaner every time I peer out the pane.

The sun goes down and they're still there.

I didn't want to overstay my welcome at the house, but after a while my girlfriend's mom caught wind of what was going down. She looked outside, closed her eyes and shook her head. "Eric," she told me. "You need to stay the night. If you leave now, you might not ever get home."

Chapter Twenty-Seven
Charlotte

I always wanted my career to involve transformative work. Growing up and moving around as much as I did through all the urban decay, I knew that doing the same things over and over and expecting different results was not going to get the job done. It is about transformation. It is about disruption. It is about revolution. It is about getting outside the box and doing new things. At least that's how I've always felt. And when I became the Real Estate Director for the City of Charlotte, North Carolina, that's the type of drive I employed to tackle the work.

When I got to the department, the old culture seemed like it could use a bit of an upgrade, and I went about rebuilding the department in order to turn around the perception of the agency. Once the culture was set, we started going after big time projects. I won't detail all of them, but I have to mention how we showed up for the city in a big way in the basketball world. See, North Carolina is hoops country. It's home to the University of North Carolina Tar Heels legendary dynasty under Dean Smith. It's the home of the Tobacco Road Rivalry between those Tarheels and the Duke University Blue Devils. It's the home state of both Michael Jordan and Stephen Curry. And, since 1988, it has been home to the NBA's Charlotte Hornets—you may remember those great 90s teams of Alonzo Mourning, Larry Johnson, and Muggsy Bogues (the shortest player in NBA history at only 5'3").

But in 2002, when the team's disgruntled owner didn't get the votes for the new public-funded stadium he wanted, he up-and-moved the franchise on down to the Bayou, where they became the New Orleans Pelicans.

And Charlotte was void of a team in a big way.

That void didn't sit well with the city. For the people and the city, it just felt like something was missing.

After a couple empty seasons—an ownership group led by Black Entertainment Television Founder Bob Johnson expressed interest in bringing a team back to Charlotte, and Bob (along with minority owner, rapper Nelly) beat out a few groups to do so, one even led by NBA legend Larry Bird.

But there was one big problem: the old arena wasn't up to snuff anymore. (It was a big reason why the old Hornets skipped town.)

And there was no existing site to build a new one.

Bob's ownership team only had thirty days to creatively conjure up a viable option or else the deal wouldn't go through.

That's where my team and I came in to help. Charlotte is unique in many ways, not the least of which is that all things real estate are handled by the real estate department, of which I was the director.

My department handled all the acquisitions. To make a long story short, I'll just tell you we put in the hours and we put in the creativity and we put in the disruptive, innovative thinking that I love—and located, worked out the details, and closed a site in 28 days.

And boom, Charlotte had an NBA basketball team again.

I'll tell you what, I was really proud of that work we all did. It took a lot of people doing a lot of great things. It took a lot of teamwork. It took a lot of courage and even a little bravado. And the results were tangible. The next season, the Charlotte Bobcats were playing and the city's morale was elevated. To get major sports back in the city made it a stronger city. And the Bobcats helped fuel the growth that spurred Charlotte to become one of the fastest growing cities in the nation.

I mean, we can all look to Oakland these days to see the downside of a major city losing its sports teams. Oakland native and NFL legend Marshawn Lynch will tell you how much losing the Raiders and A's to Vegas (and the Warriors to S.F) has hurt his city.

And if a city loses a sports team, the likelihood of getting one back is very slim. I was proud to be a part of the team that helped Charlotte get theirs back.

In addition to the Bobcats (now once again called the Hornets), my team also helped out in other ways in the fast-moving renaissance of Charlotte. We helped put together the new light rail system so the city could move beyond its outdated infrastructure and alleviate traffic congestion while providing low-income individuals more freedom of movement. We also developed a unique way to fund the creation of the NASCAR Hall of Fame, which brings a lot of pride and tourist dollars to the city. We also organized land acquisitions for new and necessary police stations, road improvements, and for freeway offramp roundabout commerce-parcels. You name it, we did it. And Charlotte became the "Buzz City" that it is today.

Chapter Twenty-Eight

Within Arm's Reach

It's fall, September or October, and I'm a sophomore at Walter L. Cohen High School getting ready for the upcoming basketball season. We are gelling as a team, and life is almost going pretty darn well.

But one day a few guys showed up on campus and picked a fight with one of my teammates. They came up during lunch and started talking shit. It was three on one. My teammate was a good guy, but he was also tough as hell and knew how to fight. And this was a *fight*. This was Ali Frazier but without any rules. It was a knock-down, drag-out. It was brutal. But in the end, my teammate won the fight.

By all accounts, we thought the feud was over.

We were wrong.

The next day we go about our business. We go to our classes, we socialize at lunch, we go to basketball practice after school. We have a good practice. Again, the team is gelling, feeling tight-knit. Practice ends and we exit the gym via the side door out into the big main yard of campus. It's about 4:30 in the afternoon, and the warm autumn sun is getting low in the sky. There are students everywhere. You've got the football team practicing, the flag twirlers are out doing their thing, the marching band is blaring their music as they get ready for the week's halftime show. And droves of other students are around too, just hanging out, talking, watching the teams practice, and mingling around. The area is packed with people, and it truly is a happy scene.

Then this car pulls up out of nowhere. Two guys jump out and start moving toward us fast. I recognize one of the guys from the fight the day before. He's looking for revenge from getting his ass beat. The other guy is a known thug he must have recruited. They were just waiting in the car for us to get out of practice.

They rush up and get in the face of my teammate they fought yesterday. He's a little up ahead of me, and it doesn't look good. With all the people and band music and commotion, I can't make out what they're saying but I don't like the tone or the body language. I run up and get closer. "What's going on here?" I ask as I approach.

There's no answer. All I hear is them yelling at each other so I get as close as I can, within arm's reach of my teammate. He and this guy in a white T-shirt are just going at each other, talking shit, threatening all kinds of things.

Then my teammate reaches in his pocket.

He pulls out a gun.

A snub-nosed '38.

He's got an ice-cold stare in his eyes like nothing I've ever seen.

"Hey man," I say, "put the gun down."

But my plea goes unheard. Before I get all the words out, the guy in the white T roars at my teammate with his own ice-cold glare. "Nigga! If you don't kill me right now, the next time I see you I'm killin' you."

I feel every eye on campus on the situation. And I'm within arm's reach of it. The gun is pointed. There's a moment where time literally stands still, then boom! My teammate pulls the trigger. He fires a shot right into the guy's chest. The guy's white T goes red faster than anything I've seen in my life. The marching band stops playing. The whistles from football practice stop. The flag twirlers stop. The crowd is one collective shock as everybody looks on, frozen. The guy in the white T doesn't scream or anything. He just hunches over and falls to the ground. My teammate proceeds to shoot him five more times—boom boom boom boom boom. I'm right there. I'm within arm's reach. I see the bullets tear into the flesh. My teammate continues to pull the trigger. No more bullets come out but the gun keeps clicking.

Then my teammate looks up from the guy and into the crowd. I look up too. It's mass chaos. Everyone scattering, taking off on a full run away from the nightmare.

I'm sixteen years old.

When I was twelve, it happened at the corner store. And now it has happened again. Me, within arm's reach of death by gun violence. Me, within arm's reach of murder. It's like some grace of God spared me or something, like some guardian angel was looking after me. I just don't know.

All I know is that I can still see that guy's white T-shirt, in an instant, turn blood red.

Needless to say, that was a very impactful day in my life. It was so monumental, in fact, that I almost forgot to include it in this book. It's like my mind, as some sort of protective measure, had made me forget about it.

And what gets me about it now (among other things), what's really sad, is that this thing happened and then things just went on as normal! I mean, we all went home that night and just came back to school the next day. There was no school cancellation for a few days while we teenagers gathered ourselves up and attempted to recover. There were no grief counselors coming to school to talk about it and help us through what happened. No one even asking us, "Hey, are you kids okay?"

The response was nothing like what happens today when there's a school shooting. It was probably nothing like what may have happened in another school district or city. This was New Orleans in the 1980s. This shit just happened. This shit was just part of life. This shit was simply part of going to school to get your education. Someone gets shot in the chest right in front of you one afternoon, and the next day you show up as if it were just something normal.

Yeah, back then we were out there on our own in our urban wilderness. There were predators. There was prey. And there were all the rest of us out on that warm autumn afternoon caught in the crossfire.

Chapter Twenty-Nine

Cleveland Here I Come!

I really liked Charlotte. I really did. I liked the city, the vibe, the people, my job. That made it a really tough decision to leave when I got recruited to go out to Cleveland, Ohio to work as the Director of Real Estate for their Port Authority. They wanted to completely redesign their waterfront area, and I was amped for the project. The city wanted it to be on par, if not better, than Chicago's. It seemed like a good challenge. It seemed like I'd get to use all that I'd learned and more. It seemed like I could be creative and bold. It seemed like an opportunity to do some good work and give the people of a different city what they'd been desiring. So I answered the call.

But when I got out to Cleveland, it quickly became apparent that things were in disarray. The longtime president of the Port Authority got ousted from his position. I wasn't on the job for more than two months when the president came up to me one morning with a sigh. "Hey, Eric—I'm sorry, but we don't have the money right now to do what we brought you here to do."

I was more than a bit confused, more than a bit disappointed. I'd just left a great gig in Charlotte to come out here and redo this waterfront. I didn't know how I could still try and pull it off, but it felt like I'd have to pull a rabbit out of my hat. "I'll tell you what," I said. "I'll reach out to the Cleveland Foundation, see what I can do."

What's The Cleveland Foundation? Well, it's the oldest community foundation in all of America—and arguably the best. It was founded back in 1914 by a successful banker and lawyer named Harris Goff who essentially left his fortune to the city of Cleveland to grow it and do whatever with it to best serve the citizenry. The Cleveland Foundation has done great work for over a century now. It is run and led and populated by good, smart people who put Cleveland first. If I was going to pull that rabbit out of my hat, I knew I needed to call upon them.

So I picked up the phone, and gave a call over there. They knew me as the Real Estate Director of the Port Authority, so they answered my ring. "Hey," I said. "I need to talk to you about my thoughts on the waterfront plan. All I need is one hour of your time and two dry-erase boards. I have my own pens. When can I come in?"

They were more than happy to oblige. In a short time, I got my meeting. I went on over and entered the room. I told them of our dire money situation on the waterfront project—and like some fifth-grade class-project I just drew out my plans on those dry-erase boards. Throughout the whole hour, I felt like I was getting my message across.

In the end, they were like, "Eric, we totally get it. We see your vision, and we like it. We'll see what we can do."

No more than two weeks passed, and the Foundation got back to me with an awarded $800,000 to follow through and complete my plan. I was jazzed. I was hyped. I felt like the citizen-value of my plan has been seen, and understood. I felt validated, like I've somehow overcome one of the biggest roadblocks of my professional life. Their generous award allowed me to bring in arguably one of the best architects in America, if not one of the best in the world, Stanton Eckstut of the Ehrenkramtz Eckstut Kuhn, who'd designed New York City's waterfront Battery Park. I was also able to bring in the former Mayor of Pittsburg, Tom Murphy, as a sort of working fellow on the project. I brought in top-notch consultants from London. I brought in the best real estate experts from in and around the Cleveland area. And we set about putting together a massive and practical and beautiful plan.

The whole thing was based solely upon what the community of Cleveland had been asking for for years. I mean, the Clevelanders were amped for it. You could feel it. It was the real-life version of some of those scenes from the great 1989 baseball film, *Major League*, when Mitch "The Wild Thing" Vaughn and Willy Mays Hays are making a run for the pennant for the down-on-their-luck Cleveland Indians.

The energy in the city was palpable.

We unveiled the project plans and the city responded so very gosh darn positively. The citizens saw everything they wanted to see, everything for which they'd been pining for so long. They saw the easy access to the water, they saw the promenades, they saw the ability to get past their dilapidated industrial port—one that had been in a state of decay for decades—morphed into a waterfront that could truly be celebrated and enjoyed by all.

Our plan gave that to the city in a big way. I mean, we hit this thing out of the park farther than a Pedro Cerano home run to beat "The Duke" and the hated Yankees in that great Cleveland baseball movie.

And, I mean, I'm not just boasting here. The area newspaper, *The Plains Dealer,* touted my leadership and work on the plan as a "Top 10 Story of the Year." It was like the field of dreams was about to be built, finally, along Cleveland's long-stale waterfront.

Yet—things that are to be do not always come to be.

With all that initial and profound excitement, I was raring to go. But for a while, nothing happened. Then, for another while nothing happened. Three months later, I found myself at my desk twiddling my thumbs and biting my fingernails. For another month I did the same. The plans were there. The money was there. The architect and the consultants and the vibe were there.

But no groundbreaking ever occurred.

I couldn't stand it any longer. One afternoon I strode into the office of the interim president of the Port Authority. He saw me enter. His face was long. I prepared for the worst. "Eric," he said, his arm on my shoulder. "I'm sorry. I'm truly sorry, but we're not going to be able to move forward on your waterfront plan."

Oh my goodness did that hurt. Oh my goodness did that sting. Oh my goodness did I just want to scream and yell like a fourteen-year-old.

But I didn't. I dug deeper.

Turns out, for some reason there was a big disconnect between the Port President and the City of Cleveland. I didn't pretend to understand why, but had spent my time in D.C; I knew politics. I knew red tape. I knew money. I knew the way of things. I knew Aristotle's words that man is a *zoon politikon,* that man is a political animal—and that, in my experience, all too often means that projects that will benefit the people do not get done.

Still, it stung like heck. Yeah, it hurt. I'd put my heart and mind and soul and *life* into giving Cleveland the waterfront park it wanted and deserved. To this day, I believe the plan I put forth was some of the best work I've ever done. It required my creativity. It required my tenacity. It required boldness and brains and bravado.

But it wasn't good enough. It was like playing a basketball game with everything you got—22 points, 12 boards, 6 assists, 4 blocks and a couple of steals—but your team still, somehow, does not find a way to win the game.

Oh well. When one door closes, I was coming to learn, another one tends to open.

Chapter Thirty

Rocks

Despite all the chaos I've spoken of in my childhood, I definitely did have four real points of grounding for me. I am extremely grateful for these blessings because I know I could not have had the life I have without them.

The first were my grandparents, Josephine and Fred Johnson. They were incredibly good people. Whenever I could get over and see them, they were incredible to me. I'd go over there and there'd be a hot meal for me. There'd be warmth. There'd be wisdom. There'd be conversation. Heck, they'd even ask me how my day was…ask me how school was going…and so much more. Their home was a sanctuary for me and just about everyone in the family.

Anyway, I just couldn't get any further in this book without giving them their due, without saying thanks. Thank you, Grandma. Thanks Grandpa. Couldn't have done it all without you.

The second aspect of my young life that provided grounding and moral guidance was the Catholic church. I was an altar boy. The priests and the rites and the structure was good for me. The Good Book was good for me. Going to church during that time in my life was a form of comfort, a small sampling of peace. It helped lay my moral foundation—and I looked forward to it every Sunday. I'd usually take the early mass, the one at 7:30 in the morning. That was my favorite, but if I couldn't get there in time, the 9:00 service worked too. I learned so very much from them. Each and every Sunday was very, very good. (Besides, serving as an altar boy during the early mass allowed my friends and I to go to the movies to watch kung fu, Godzilla and horror movies in the afternoon.)

Third, I had school. School was my rock. No matter where I lived, no matter what was going on at home, no matter if my mom woke me up from slumber to beat me for forgetting to do the dishes, I had school. My vivid memories really come through my schools, and I can still think back and track my age and all those places we lived in by what school I was attending.

By the time I got to middle school at Sophie B. Wright, I knew I was a good student. I had a growing knowledge that education was my path. I loved my classes. I loved the books. I loved all of my teachers. I just loved learning. Learning, the stability of a classroom. Get the lesson, take notes, study up, ace the test. It was a source of pride, a sense of identity.

By high school I got into student government and became Vice President of student government, class of 1982 at Walter. L. Cohen. My GPA was always good. I felt the high regard from my teachers and from my peers. This gave me a sense of belonging that, funny or sad as this may sound, I never felt like I got at home.

I loved school so much that during the summers in high school I would attend Loyola University Upward Bound program. Some neighborhood friends and I would live on campus, attend classes, and play basketball. It was there that I received my earliest intentions on attending college.

My fourth point of grounding was the New Orleans Public Library. Libraries were a real constant in my life. They were neighborhood-based uptown, and they were places where I really grew. I made sure to stop at one or another of them on my way home from school so I could do homework, read, and just marvel at the thousands of books on the shelves. I just always thought the library was a cool place to be.

So yeah, I just didn't want to make it out like I had no positive places of moral grounding growing up in that often-nightmarish childhood I've told you about. I didn't have a lot, but in my grandparents, the church, school, and the libraries, I was afforded peace, guidance, positive community, and grounding.

And I needed it.

Because we all need it.

No one in this life can do it all by themself. Lone wolves in our society really don't exist. And even if they do exist, they rarely thrive.

We need our rocks. Just like a kelp forest out in the ocean, without being anchored down to that rock, all those leaves would just float away aimlessly at sea. It's the same for people—we need a few rocks to ground us. Sometimes we need to go seek them out, seek out our good people and good places.

I sincerely hope—no matter how young or old you are, no matter how much money you have or don't have—that you have some good places of morality and grounding. We all need them. No matter if you live in the suburbs or you live in the projects, find good people and places that help you recognize right and wrong.

They say "it takes a village." Even if your village is only a few people, or only a certain place or two, that can be enough. For, without them, we human beings have a way of getting pretty lost pretty quick.

Chapter Thirty-One
The Big D

So yeah, I moved around a lot professionally. Sometimes, like in Cleveland, the rug got pulled out from under me, but mostly my moves have been by design. I like to keep going, I'm not a "stay in the same job for 10 years" type guy. It goes back to my childhood. It goes back to reading the *Countering the Conspiracy to Destroy Black Boys*. It goes back to the chip on the shoulder, the constant feeling of needing to play catch up, the constant desire to continue to accelerate, to improve, to disrupt, and to create positive change. With all the moving around, I've developed my niche as a leader. Whether it's the non-profit sector, the public sector, or the private sector, I have worked on transformative urban development projects and issues in the Northeast, Midwest, South, and Southeastern regions of the United States. I have served in key positions in economic development, housing and urban improvement, and community development policy and management. I'm the, "If you want to get this fixed fast, I'm your guy" guy. I come in, I stabilize the situation, I get the project done, and then I move onto the next place where I can help out the most. I'm a disruption-change person.

That's how I got to Dallas, Texas. My old friend from Washburn State, T.C. Broadnax, and I were on the phone one day. He's the City Manager of Dallas. "Eric," he said. "We need a gunslinger out here. We need *you*."

I was kind of flattered by the compliment. I mean, I like a good Western flick, I liked watching Brett Favre sling it around the gridiron. But I wasn't sure. "I don't know, T.C. I'm being recruited by Tyler Perry to redevelop his movie studio project over in Atlanta."

"No, Big E. This is good work, and I've got my hands full. Come do it."

I had to make a decision. The iconic black actor, Tyler Perry, had bought a portion of an old military base to create a big studio in Atlanta. I was recruited to lead the redevelopment of the former military base adjacent to the studio. I asked myself a question: do I do some kind of redevelopment glamor work for a Hollywood A lister or do I go and help some regular people in Dallas as the Chief of Economic Development?

I slept on it, then chose the latter.

Still, I had to wade carefully into the political scene in Dallas. Everyone had their own personal agendas. But T.C. was all about trying to really set a new direction for the city, in particular with economic development and housing planning, and I liked that. It was disruptive and creative, and I was in. We started with corporate relocations, creating an economic development policy, affordable housing measures, and upgrading the city's permitting processes.

There was behind-the-scenes push back. There was negativity. There were forces trying to come after what T.C. and I were doing. But they didn't know who they were dealing with. I'm not a fearful guy, so they weren't going to intimidate me. I interacted with the business community, the real estate community, and the elected officials. I went into Big D and T.C and I (along with some other great team members) did some great stuff. I won't bore you with the policy details or the nitty gritty here, but I have to say that it felt pretty dang full-circle to work in the professional space with my old teammate from Washburn State.

And there was this funny little phone call one day.

It was kind of a rare coincidence, but the Mayor of Dallas at the time shared the same name with me: he was Eric Johnson, I was Eric Johnson. One day I was sitting in my office, the panoramic view of downtown outside my window as I was getting ready for a committee meeting later that day. My assistant rushed into my office. "Hey, Dr. J, (yeah, that's what they called me) there's a call coming in for you. It's from Washington."

I half laughed. "Like from the White House?" I asked.

"Uh, *yes* actually. It *is* the White House."

I sat up straight in my chair. "Well, yeah. I think I'll take the call."

The phone rang. I let it ring once or twice before I answered. A female voice was on the other end: "Yes, this is the White House calling on behalf of the President of the United States. We are trying to reach Eric Johnson."

"Um, yes," I managed, "this is he."

It was as if she didn't recognize my voice or she was expecting something different. "Um—are you the mayor?"

Dang. "No, no. I'm the Chief of Economic Development and Housing."

"Well, that's a coincidence. The White House is trying to reach the mayor."

"But I'm Eric Johnson too," I say, "if the President needs to talk to me, I can talk to him!"

The other end went silent for a while.

I let out a laugh. "No, I'm just joking," I said finally. "I figured you were looking for the mayor. Let me give you his number, I have it right here…."

I gave the White House the *other* Eric Johnson's number. Then I hung up the phone, chuckled a little bit about life's funny coincidences, and continued to prepare for the committee meeting.

Chapter Thirty-Two

Down Under

After my time in Dallas and earning an MBA from the University of Tennessee, I accepted the position to become the President and CEO of Aeon—a nonprofit-housing and real-estate development organization working in and around Minneapolis. That's what I do now. I love the work, and I love the challenge. We own and operate roughly 6,000 housing units in the Twin Cities area, housing about 17,000 low-income residents. It's a challenging and very rewarding position.

Upon getting to town and taking on the new role, though, it was a tough time in Minneapolis. The city was just coming off the murder of George Floyd and all the social unrest that followed. The pandemic had taken its toll as well, and the eviction moratorium—which created a situation where people really didn't have to pay rent anymore because no one had the power to evict tenants for it—was a test for the organization to say the least. I mean, we lost 63% of our annual revenue due to non-payment of rent. The lenders still wanted their mortgage payments but our properties simply were not cash flowing. Property maintenance and capital improvement needs were going unmet, and crime and security costs were skyrocketing. There was resident discontent. Tenant rights organizations, elected officials, and the media were up in arms. Needless to say, it was a tough reality trying to operate, develop, and preserve affordable housing in the Twin Cities.

But it has provided some opportunities as well. In getting to deal with these issues, I had the chance to go to Toronto to speak about the housing challenges extant in Minneapolis and the United States as a whole. It was a great opportunity to share my message in a beautiful city amongst intellectual and driven people. I went for it. I gave it my all. I spoke from the heart, speaking heavily about the challenges of the social and economic issues of affordable housing in America—and how the system as currently designed is broken, incapable of meeting the affordable housing challenge in the United States.

It was intense.

And would you know it? The speech was received so well that I was invited to speak somewhere even bigger on the issue. I was invited all the way down to Australia to give an address at the Power Housing National Conference as the international keynote speaker.

I was beyond honored—I accepted the invite in about .243 seconds.

I knew I could help. I mean, Australia was (and still is) in the midst of a mass urbanization movement. And there have long been problems with the people in power clashing with the indigenous Aboriginal population. As in our country, there is a widespread wealth gap; the rich are getting richer and the poor are getting poorer as the middle class erodes. A true housing crisis has developed—and Australia has just recently passed a $10 billion housing initiative with the aim of basically building as many affordable units as possible over a five-year period. To get the best return on investment, they asked for my perspective, for "the American perspective." I was more than willing to fly down there to share some of my insights. I was thinking, "Wow, this is wild. The little boy from the streets of uptown New Orleans is going to Australia, huh?"

I looked at a globe, spun it around. Australia truly is an island bordered by the Pacific, Indian, and Southern Oceans way down in the southern hemisphere. From Minneapolis it would take 22 hours to fly there, and the time difference would be a staggering seventeen hours ahead. When I got there, it would already be tomorrow, and I would be a world away from anything I knew.

Except for affordable housing. That, I knew.

And that's why I was invited down there. I had been invited down there because of my speech in Toronto and because of everything I'd done up until this point in my life. All the homes I lived in as a child. All the schools I'd been to and all the degrees I'd earned. My Presidential Management Fellowship. Working with the New Orleans City Council. Even the lessons I'd learned in basketball and in the Army. Everything I had done had led to right now.

In addition to the keynote address, I was later informed, they wanted me to come out a few days early and travel in-country to meet with a few organizations, CEOs, and policy-makers to talk about affordable housing and all that entails—from Sidney to Melbourne and inland to the capital city of Canberra.

Needless to say, I was feeling a little bit nervous about the whole thing.

But I was also excited.

And also very proud.

I listened to some Hip Hop and R&B as I got my bags packed, and got ready to head Down Under.

I arrived in Sydney. It's a beautiful city—the iconic bridge over the bay, the iconic Opera House with its wing-like architecture, the beaches, the whole thing. It reminds me of San Francisco, our City on the Bay, but just a little cleaner and crisper. The people are friendly. The people are cool. But pretty early on, something hit me: I was the only person of color around. It's a city of around five million, and I seem like the only "black fella" around. I mean, I'm coming from one of the whitest states in the U.S. in Minnesota, but it hits me hard to be the lone black face in a sea of white faces. Plus, I'm taller than pretty much everyone too.

So yeah, I stood out. People were looking at me out of the corner of their eyes as I walked down the street. "This is different," I kept saying to myself. "This is different." I carried on—taking in the sights and just walking around the new land with curiosity and excitement.

I spent a few days in Sydney meeting with various community organizations, touring their properties and gaining an understanding of what they do compared to how we do it in the U.S. I saw vast differences in how they build versus how we build; basically, they build their affordable housing as a for-sale product, while America tends to do it as a rental product.

After my days in Sydney, I flew inland to Canberra, the capital, to meet with CEOs and hold roundtable discussions. We talked about the comparable challenges we all faced—and how to get the best results, how to help the most people. I also did a series of smaller workshop groups, discussions with various developers and affordable housing gurus of the area. We talked about residence issues, nonpayment issues, crime and drugs and skin color and socioeconomics and everything under the sun.

As part of my work back stateside with Aeon, I had been doing a YouTube series called "Chats from Home", about the types of things we do and the strategies we employ to get them done. The Australians I met with had largely viewed these videos, were familiar with their content, and they asked me a lot of follow-up questions about them— especially on how to deal with social issues and challenges.

Yeah, myself personally and Aeon as an organization had dealt with more than our fair share of challenging properties. One of the complexes we own is Huntington Place Apartments, the second largest multi-family housing complex in Minnesota. It consists of about 834 units that house roughly 2,800 low-income residents. It was purchased by Aeon in 2020, literally right before the pandemic hit, to avoid the mass eviction of the residents—more people than many small towns in America.

The property is located in Brooklyn Park, Minnesota, and when we acquired it, the grounds were in bad shape. Imagine an apartment complex that had 30+ years of deferred maintenance and improvement needs that had been sort of taken over by gang-type activities. It almost reminded me of Park Chester growing up—all the drug use, the shootings, the resident's dissatisfaction, the whole lot. If you were to look at the local newspaper and do a scan of Huntington Place Apartments, you would see the truth. It was a problem. When Aeon bought it, the plan was to acquire it through a bridge loan—which basically means a short-term loan for five years, and then at the end of the five years, we would refinance. We tried everything in terms of trying to refinance the property. We scoured the country working with Baker Tilly, which is a nationally-renowned finance consulting firm. We also worked with Capital One, who did some analysis for us. But the problem was just the sheer negativity coming from the property; along with tenants simply not paying their rent, there was all the gang and drug stuff. We were in a forbearance mode, really unable to pay the mortgage.

To gain better footing, we worked hard to calm down the security challenges at the property. We hired a security team that rivaled a special forces unit and put up a massive fence around the property. Still, we could not move the needle to secure any financing. Interest rates were up, inflation was rearing its head, and it was really not working well for us. The property had something like a 15-25% vacancy rate, so from a cash flow perspective it was simply not working. And we knew if we faltered on the property, 2,800 people would be out on the streets.

But we were running out of steam and running out of options.

Enter my trip to Australia. See, the world is vast but it is also quite small. I went all the way from Minneapolis, Minnesota to Sydney, Australia and then over to Canberra, where I happened to come face-to-face with the individual from Morgan Stanley who was overseeing the loan for Huntington Place. It was surreal; I mean, I had no idea he was going to be there. It was a gift—I had the opportunity to spend a significant amount of time talking with him about the challenges we were facing and everything we had been doing to hold onto the property. I told him how we'd secured $10 million from the state of Minnesota and how we had a 4 million-dollar congressional appropriation—and that we were working to access those dollars to continue to hold the property. I looked him in the eye. "Look," I said. "I really need your guys' help on this thing. We're out of steam and options here."

I gave them the context that I don't think they were truly aware of in terms of what we had been doing and the level of energy we were putting into the property. It was somewhat uncomfortable to talk about being behind on our mortgage payments, but all I really asked for was his ability to be patient with us.

To my surprise, I reached the guy. Morgan Stanley communicated that they would hold with us. They didn't want 2,800 people out on the streets either, and they showed some real heart. They showed some real grit. Their mission as community-impact investors really came through, and it was an admirable moment.

And all it took was me going halfway around the world to have an impromptu face-to-face! It really was a miracle; our year-end board meeting was about to take place. Had I not had that conversation, the topic could have been about us turning in the keys on the property, and mass evictions. And while the future of the property was still up in the air, I was able to play my part in trying to find a solution so we could continue to fight the good fight.

But back to why I was in Australia in the first place: my keynote address. My talk was about the challenges of inequality in housing in the United States—in particular, the historical challenges in housing for African Americans and tying it to the issues Australia has had with their indigenous Aboriginal population. I spoke on the levels of inequalities in the U.S that date back to the 1930s and the latter days of Jim Crow—hoping to help improve Australian policies going forward.

I walked up to the podium and caught myself just looking out across the few-hundred people in attendance. And again, it hit me—

I'm the only person of color. My mind went back to being the kid who grew up in New Orleans. I felt so fortunate to be right here right now, having grown up in that environment, proving myself, making my own way. My mind flashed to all the people I grew up with. I got this feeling that today, in Australia, I am representing every one of them who didn't make it. I was about to speak on the issues rampant in affordable housing—and the tactics of exclusion in United States housing policy that set the stage for the African American experience and the social and economic challenges that plagued myself, my family, and my friends growing up.

The people I'm representing didn't not make it because they were bad people or because they weren't smart—only because their environment snagged them up and held them back from reaching their full social and economic potential. I was up on the podium in front of the audience, and got a weird feeling: I had this feeling of survivor's remorse, a sense of feeling equally proud and sad at the same time. I thought back to my time at Sophie B. Wright Middle School and Walter L. Cohen High School. *Man*, I said to myself as I looked out at the audience. *Life is crazy*.

And then I started my speech. I spoke from the heart. I spoke from experience, and I spoke for an improved future.

I can tell the audience was rapt. I felt eye contact from the entire room. I saw nodding heads. I felt the energy. I talked about the levels of inequality in the history of American housing, and how our country has struggled to move beyond it. I talked about housing policies that sought to keep African Americans suppressed in their opportunity to buy homes and to create wealth. I can tell that the audience hadn't really ever heard of the things I was talking about, and I felt a sort of collective shock at the history of American housing I was revealing. I basically plead for Australia to *not do* what we have done in the United States, urging the Aussies to not restrict opportunities for minorities and people of color.

I finished my speech and the applause was loud. The follow-up questions were good, apt, and I answered to the best of my ability. Then there was more applause. As I walked down from the podium, it was an all-time moment in my life. I was in a sea of people and all I could think about was the courage of that young boy in that photograph (on the cover of this book). All his challenges and disappointments. Being down but never out. Not following the crowd. Goal setting and living life's lessons. The endless pursuit of excellence and education. Not allowing environmental forces to dictate his outcome. Believing in himself.

That little boy's journey is not complete, because my journey is not yet complete. And as I head into the next chapter in my life, I want to take this moment to acknowledge my younger self. To say thank you for your vision, your insight, and your strength. That little boy inside of me is so proud of me—of who I am today. And that little boy inside of me has been leading the way the entire time. He was, and still is, my origin of strength.

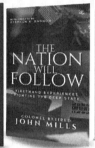

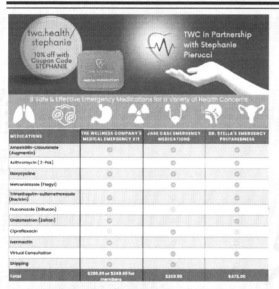

Made in the USA
Columbia, SC
10 August 2024

425cf00b-6ab8-4b3e-88da-e9e728118082R01